RICKY PONTING

AUSTRALIAN CRICKETER

MR VIVEK KUMAR PANDEY SHAMBHUNATH

ISBN 979-888555164-9

Short biography of Ricky Ponting and about life.During writing this book no character & no religious are harmed written by Mr Vivek Kumar Pandey. winner youngest writer award 1st rank in india 2020.He is only one writer can publish 760+ own book that was greatest successfull in his life.This All Credit Goes To My Super Hero Daddy.

Contents

Foreword

Author biography in English :MY NAME IS VIVEK KUMAR PANDEY . I WAS BORN IN 30 SEP 2002,I AM FROM SURAT GUJARAT INDIA.MY DREAM WAS TO BE GOOD WRITERS ,MY FAMILY SUPPORTED ME TO SUCCESSFUL AND I CAN DO IT MY SELF.How do I write? That is a question, I believe, that can be honestly answered by me."CELEBRATING YOUNGEST WRITER AWARD WINNER IN GUJARAT 1ST RANK" MR PANDEY JI . I may think I did a good job writing something . The reader is the one who decides the quality of my writing. I do find writing to be natural to me and therefore find it to be a real challenge. My trick as a challenged writer is to do the best I can and know that I am happy with the final outcome. It may take a while to do my best and there may be quite a few problems I run into along the way.

I am not a greedy person those who are thinking about me and my self I never tried it anyone people suffering from sadness ,I trying to get promoted people suffering from happiness and joy in your Life Time. Now in current situation in India and also world people are unemployed and have no many but our indian governor help to people to get free food from ration card , i also take part in leadership team ,i am Motivational speaker , Film script writer. There was my two dream firstly writer and secondly actor & also my own film is upcoming soon i done almost completely completed script for my film .I AM GOING TO SAY WORD OF HEART TOUCH OUT PLEASE READ IT" , firstly i thanks my father he supports me in this field they always getting inspired me by own his words and behavior ,they always said that he was a biggest person in the world in future and also they purchase fruit and chocolate for me in anytime & anyway , firstly my father buy him then call me Vivek you want a chocolate i will say yes papa but how many tell me ,papa: you tell me how much i buy him i told 1 or 2 chocolate but my father purchase whole the boxes of chocolate and they get suprised me. MY FATHER WAS BORN IN " 20 SEPTEMBER" 1971 IN INDIA.

1) MY FATHER FAVORITE CLOTHES IS KURTA PAIJMA AND ALSO STYLES SHOE

2) FAVORITE SINGER IS KISHORE DA

3) FAVORITE STATE GUJARAT AND KOLKATA , HIS VILLAGE IN BIHAR

4) FAVORITE COLOR BLACK AND WHITE

THEY ALSO LOVE cricket like IPL and one day t-20 .they also like watching a News daily and heard the song daily ,they also interested in tik tok video but in current time tik tok is banned in india but also few videos are in you tube. In lockdown time my family and me very enjoy day daily. my father play daily ludo with his sister and son, daughter.they always loved tea and coffee anytime call me "। वविंक थोडा़ चाय बनाओना वविंक तुम्हारे हाथ का चाय अच्छा लगता है". I make it tea for my father but some reason after the April to june they are suffering from fever and cough , weakness on 6 June 2020 my father death. they not told me say bye bye his life. After death of 6 June on 10 june my mom and dad anniversary.but my father is Best in the world they can do anything for me please take care of father and respect it of your parents.

CHAPTER ONE

Ricky Ponting

- *Ricky Ponting*

1. Disclaimer : During writing this book no character & no religious are harmed written by Mr Vivek Kumar Pandey.

Ricky Thomas Ponting AO (born 19 December 1974) is an Australian cricket coach, commentator, and former cricketer. Ponting was captain of the Australian national team during its "golden era", between 2004 and 2011 in Test cricket and 2002 and 2011 in One Day Internationals (ODIs) and is the most successful captain in international cricket history, with 220 victories in 324 matches with a winning rate of 67.91%. He is widely considered to be one of the best batsmen of the modern era and in December 2006 reached the highest rating achieved by a Test batsman for 50 years, although this was surpassed by Steve Smith in December 2017. He stands second in the list of cricketers by number of international centuries scored behind Sachin Tendulkar.

Domestically Ponting played for his home state of Tasmania as well as Tasmania's Hobart Hurricanes in Australia's domestic Twenty20 competition, the Big Bash League. He played as a specialist right-handed batsman, an excellent slip fielder, as well as a very occasional bowler. He led Australia to their second 5–0 Ashes win as well as victory at the 2003 and 2007 Cricket World Cups and was also a member of the 1999 World Cup winning team under Steve Waugh. He led Australia to consecutive ICC Champions Trophy victory in 2006 and 2009. Combative and at times a controversial captain, statistically he is one of the most successful Test captains of all time, with 48 victories in 77 Tests between 2004 and 31 December 2010. As a player, Ponting is the only cricketer in history to be involved in 100 Test victories and was involved in the most ODI victories as a player, with 262 wins, having played in over 160 Tests and 370 ODIs.

A prolific batter, Ponting is Australia's leading run-scorer in Test and ODI cricket. He was named "Cricketer of the Decade 2000" was named in the country's best Ashes XI in a Cricket Australia poll in 2017 and in July 2018 he was inducted into the ICC Hall of Fame. He is the current assistant coach of the Australian national men's cricket team, having been appointed to the role in February 2019.

Ponting announced his retirement from Test cricket in November 2012, the day before playing in his final Test against South Africa; this was his 168th and last Test appearance, equalling the Australian record held by Steve Waugh. He retired with a Test batting average of 51.85, although he continued to play cricket around the world until 2013.

- *Birth and life*

Born in Launceston, Tasmania, on 19 December 1974, Ricky Ponting is the eldest of Graeme and Lorraine Ponting's four children. Graeme was "a good club cricketer" and played Australian rules football, while Lorraine was a state vigoro champion.His uncle Greg Campbell played Test cricket for Australia in 1989 and 1990. Ponting's parents first lived in Prospect 4.1 km (2.5 mi) south of city centre; however, they moved into the working-class area of Newnham, 6 km (3.7 mi) north of central Launceston.

After marrying his long-time girlfriend, law student Rianna Cantor, in June 2002, Ponting credited her as the reason for his increased maturity. The couple have three children.

- *Junior ranks*

Introduced to cricket by father Graeme and uncle Greg Campbell, Ponting played for the Mowbray Under–13s team at the age of 11 in 1985–86. In January 1986, he took part in the five-day annual Northern Tasmania junior cricket competition. After scoring four centuries in a week, bat manufacturer Kookaburra gave Ponting a sponsorship contract while in just eighth grade mainly on the back of these four centuries. Ponting took this form into the Under-16s week-long competition less than a month later, scoring an even century on the final day.Ted Richardson, the former head of the Northern Tasmanian Schools Cricket Association said: "Ricky is certainly the equal of David Boon at this level.

Australian Rules football was also a big part of Ponting's sporting life, and is a keen follower of the North Melbourne Kangaroos. During the winter he played junior football for North Launceston and up until he was 14, it could have become a possible sporting option. This was before he broke the humerus in his right arm playing for North Launceston Under–17s as a 13-year-old. Ponting's arm was so badly damaged, it had to be pinned. Told to endure a 14-week lay-off, he never played competitive football again.

During Tasmanian Sheffield Shield matches at the NTCA Ground (Northern Tasmanian Cricket Association Ground), Ponting helped out with the scoreboard, thereby surrounding himself with international cricketers. After leaving school at the end of year 10 in 1990, he began work as a groundsman at Scotch Oakburn College, a private school in Launceston. In 1991 the Northern Tasmanian Cricket Association sponsored Ponting to attend a fortnight's training at the Australian Cricket Academy in Adelaide. The two weeks turned into a full two-year sponsorship as he was said to be the best 17-year-old batsman Academy coach Rod Marsh had ever seen.

Playing five games for Tasmania for the 1992 Under–19 carnival in Perth, Ponting scored 350 runs, earning him selection in the 13-man national Under–19 development squad for the upcoming tour of South Africa—the first Australian cricket team to make an official tour to the country since Bill Lawry's team in 1970.

- *Early Australian domestic career*

Ponting made his first-class debut for Tasmania in November 1992, when just 17 years and 337 days old, becoming the youngest Tasmanian to play in a Sheffield Shield match. However, he had to wait until 1995 before making his ODI debut, during a quadrangular tournament in New Zealand in a match against South Africa. His Test debut followed shortly after, when selected for the first Test of the 1995 home series against Sri Lanka in Perth, in which he scored 96. He lost his place in the national team several times in the period before early-1999, due to lack of form and discipline, before becoming One Day International captain in early-2002 and Test captain in early 2004. After scoring 114 not out in club match against Riverside, Ponting became the youngest player to appear for Tasmania in a Sheffield Shield match, breaking Boon's record by 14 days.

In November 1992, with Ponting just 17 years and 337 days, he went to the crease at number four against South Australia at the Adelaide Oval. Despite scoring 56 in a 127-run partnership with Boon, he could not prevent a defeat, scoring just four in Tasmania's second innings. In his first match in Tasmania, this time against New South Wales, Ponting contributed 32 and 18 in a draw. He followed this up with 25 against Western Australia in a narrow loss. His first match in Sydney also marked the debut of future Australian opening bowler Glenn McGrath. His subsequent century also meant that Ponting became the youngest Tasmanian to score a first-class century at 18 years and 40 days, eclipsing Boon's record of 19 years and 356 days.After scoring another half century, Ponting scored back to back centuries against Western Australia on Australia's fastest wicket in Perth.He became the youngest batsmen in Shield history to score twin centuries in a match. After setting a goal of scoring 500 runs in the season, he ended up scoring 781 at 48.81. After season's end, Ponting played seven four-day games for the Australian Academy, scoring 484 runs at 96.70, even though he was still only 18.

Speculation ignited that Ponting was an outsider to join the Australian squad on their 1993 tour to England. Despite Ponting's reluctance to weigh into the debate, Tasmanian coach Greg Shipperd thought he could handle the experience.

The selectors ended up choosing Western Australian batsman Damien Martyn for the tour, with Ponting selected in the academy squad captained by Justin Langer, which toured India and Sri Lanka for seven games in August–September 1993. Australian success was limited, with only several wins. No batsman scored a century, despite Ponting reaching 99 not out in a one-day game in Colombo. He finished the tour second highest in the aggregates, behind Langer.Before the start of the 1993–94 Sheffield Shield season, Ponting stated that he wanted to score 1000 runs for the season.In Tasmania's final match of the season, they needed to defeat South Australia outright to qualify for the final. Set 366 in 102 overs, Ponting scored 161 in a 290-run partnership that ended with Tasmania needing just 41 runs for victory. Despite Tasmania losing four quick wickets, they won with four wickets in hand. Disappointingly for Ponting, he could not repeat the performance in the final against New South Wales, scoring just one and 28, as Tasmania were defeated by an innings and 61 runs. The season saw Ponting score 965 runs at 48.25, close to his 1000 run goal.

A month after the final, he was again selected for the academy squad for three limited overs matches against a touring Indian team. Queenslander Stuart Law captained the Australian side that included former Australian keeper Rod Marsh. In Australia's victory in Canberra he top scored with 71 and before scoring 52 in victory in Sydney. The last match was also successful for the home team, with Ponting not required to bat.

Ponting started his 1994–95 campaign with a century against eventual Shield champions Queensland in Brisbane, impressing Queensland captain Allan Border, "He's just an outstanding prospect", Border said. Speculation again arose that Ponting could become a candidate for the upcoming tour to the West Indies. When Tasmania played Western Australia at Bellerive Oval on 4 November 1994, Ponting scored 211. The century was his fifth successive against Western Australia; Sir Donald Bradman is the only other batsman to score five consecutive centuries against another state in Shield history. Ten days after the double century, Ponting was named in the Australian XI to take on England at Bellerive Oval—in a match that was used as practice before the upcoming series in the West Indies. Future Australian representatives Matthew Hayden, Langer, Greg Blewett and Martyn were also selected. In a drawn match Ponting compiled a half-century.

A fourth team was introduced to the World Series Cup in 1994–95—Australia A—for the only time. Australian captain Mark Taylor was not a fan of this change as many fans supported Australia A rather than the national team. Despite the negative feedback it gave Ponting a chance on the international stage. Playing for Australia A, he scored 161 runs at 26.83 with one half-century.

- *1995–1999 International career*

Ponting's domestic performances were rewarded when he was selected for the Australian ODI team to play in all the matches in the 1995 New Zealand Centenary quadrangular tournament in New Zealand, that also included South Africa and India. Ponting made his debut against South Africa at number six in the batting order. He scored one from six balls, as Australia successfully chased South Africa's target on a difficult batting track. Australia secured another victory in their next match, this time against New Zealand in Auckland, where Ponting scored 10 not out, after coming to wicket late in the innings. His highest series score came in the third International where Australia lost to India in Dunedin. Ponting was promoted to number three in the batting order and responded by scoring 62 from 92 balls. The innings was scored without a boundary and was based on "deft placement and judicious running." The loss failed to stop Australia from appearing in the final against New Zealand in Auckland. Ponting returned to number six and was seven not out when the winning runs were scored. He finished the series with 80 runs at 40 and strike rate of 71.42 runs per hundred balls.

- Greg Shipperd publicly suggested that Ponting could be selected as a reserve wicket-keeper for the upcoming West Indies tour, despite not keeping-wicket for Tasmania. However, he had kept wicket in pre-season matches and during centre wicket practice. In any case Ponting was selected as a specialist batsman. "... It was like all my birthdays had come at once. I had some reservations about making my Test debut against arguably the best fast bowling attack in the world", Ponting later said.

The West Indies had been cricket's powerhouse for close to two decades and teams included many feared fast bowlers. Before the tour, Australian captain Mark Taylor thought the last Test batting vacancy was possibly between Ponting and Justin Langer. "Ricky Ponting is more the stroke player while Justin is the tough man. It depends on what we need at the time but you can probably say Ricky has his neck in front because he's been on this tour of New Zealand", Taylor said.

- Rod Marsh believed Ponting's attitude and fearless approach could tear the West Indies apart. Nevertheless, Ponting did not expect to be selected. Steve Waugh noted that Ponting would "not be intimidated by the West Indians' inevitable waist-to-chin length." During the series, Ponting said the current crop of bowlers were not "of the same high class" that opposition teams had come to expect from the West Indies.

Ponting was selected for the third ODI on 12 March 1995 at Queen's Park Oval, when Mark Waugh missed out through injury. Ponting—batting at three—was involved in a 59-run partnership with Steve Waugh; however, he was dismissed for 43 when he lifted an attempted pull shot. Mark Waugh returned for the next match and Ponting was subsequently dropped until he replaced an out-of-form David Boon in the fifth and final match, where Ponting got a second-ball duck. In a three-day warm-up match ahead of the

Tests, Ponting scored 19, with Greg Blewett scoring a century and Langer compiling a half-century.

The performance was not enough for Ponting to force his way into the Test side; though, Australia did regain the Frank Worrell Trophy for the first time in 20 years, winning the series 2–1. When Ponting returned to Launceston in June 1995, Tasmania's TAB announced him as their part-time ambassador. He then undertook a tour to England with the Young Australians; a team that included fellow Tasmanian Shaun Young. It also included five future Test batsmen: Matthew Hayden, Matthew Elliott, Martin Love, Justin Langer and Stuart Law. Despite not batting as well as he "would have liked", Ponting returned to Australia with the fourth highest batting average—48.73.

Tasmania toured Zimbabwe for five games ahead of the 1995–96 Sheffield Shield. Ponting struggled, aggregating 99 runs at a modest 24.75. By the end of October, he had signed a contract with the Australian Cricket Board, along with 22 other Australian cricketers.

He opened the batting with Boon in Tasmania's first match of the Sheffield Shield season, scoring 20 and 43. Ahead of the following match against Queensland in Hobart, Ponting set himself a goal of scoring a century in each innings; a feat he achieved in a high-scoring draw. His form continued against the touring Sri Lankans in a one-day game in Devonport, scoring 99. He scored another century against the same opposition in Launceston. During the match, the public address system at the NTCA Ground announced that Ponting was making his Test debut against Sri Lanka in Perth on 8 December. The following morning saw local newspaper The Examiner headline: "He's Ricky Ponting, he's ours ... and he's made it! Tassie's batting star will play in his first Test." Marsh continued his praise of Ponting, who replaced a dropped Blewett. "I have no doubt Ricky will be trying to get 100 in his first Test game. And I hope he does. You'd back him to. If Ricky carries with him the same attitude that he has seen him succeed at First-class cricket to the next level there is no reason why he will not continue to score."

Sri Lanka batted first and scored 251, before Ponting—batting at number five due to Steve Waugh's absence through injury—arrived at the crease with Australia at a comfortable 3/422. He started nervously, edging his first ball past first slip for a boundary from off-spinner Muttiah Muralitharan. When Ponting reached 96, Chaminda Vaas hit Ponting high on his thigh and was given out leg before wicket.

Many members of the crowd and media argued it was an incorrect decision due to excessive height. He combined with Stuart Law, also playing on debut, for a partnership of 121. This was only the ninth ever century partnership by debutants in Test cricket. "I've got mixed emotions about my knock at the moment. 96 is a good score but it would have been nice to get a 100", Ponting said after the innings. "Once I struck a few in the middle of the bat, and I spent some time in the middle I tried to relax and enjoy it, just savour the moment." Australia won the match by an innings. In the second Test in Melbourne on Boxing Day, he scored a "compact" 71 in his only innings, combining for a century stand with Steve Waugh. He also took the wicket of Asanka Gurusinha in Sri Lanka's first innings amidst four economical overs.

However, Ponting's performance was overshadowed by Australian umpire Darrell Hair no-balling Muralitharan for throwing on seven occasions, increasing tensions between the two teams. Ponting's fellow Tasmanian Boon retired after the Third Test, and Ponting's performances were not as strong at number six in the batting order, managing six and 20. Australia won yet again, sweeping the series 3–0, and Ponting was in full praise of Boon. "I would have hated to be the first person to come through from Launceston and make it but he has proved it can be done", Ponting said a year before his Test debut. Ponting ended his debut Test series with 193 runs at 48.25.

Though Ponting's appearances for Tasmania continued to be limited, he was still able to top the 1995–96 season averages with 59.50. He played in all ten games of the World Series ODI Cup played between Australia, Sri Lanka and the West Indies after the Test series.Ponting started the series at number four but moved up a position midway through the season, after opener Michael Slater was dropped. He broke through for his maiden ODI century in his 12th match, scoring 123 from 138 balls against Sri Lanka at the MCG. However, the effort was not enough to prevent Sri Lanka from victory. Ponting ended his first home ODI tournament with 341 runs at 34.10, including one century and three fifties, as Australia ended as series champions.

- *1996 World Cup*

A Tamil Tiger bombing in Colombo coupled with death threats to some members of the team forced Australia to forfeit their scheduled 1996

Cricket World Cup match against Sri Lanka in Colombo. Ponting batted in the number three position for the entire tournament, and scored six in Australia's opening match victory over Kenya. He continued to be inconsistent with scores of 12 and 33 against India and Zimbabwe, before becoming the youngest batsman to score a World Cup century, when he scored 102 runs from 112 balls against the West Indies in Jaipur.

Ponting wore a cap instead of a helmet to show the West Indians that he did not fear them. The effort was not enough, as Australia lost by four wickets. Australia finished second in their group and faced New Zealand in the quarter-finals. He scored 41 followed by a 15-ball duck in a semi-final victory against the West Indies, as Australia staggered to 8/207. Australia appeared to be heading out of the tournament when the Caribbean team reached 2/165, but a sudden collapse saw Australia win by six runs in the last over. Ponting scored 45 from 73 balls in the final at the Gaddafi Stadium in Lahore, which Australia lost to Sri Lanka. Ponting ended his first World Cup campaign with 229 runs at 32.71.

In August, Australia played in the Singer Cup in Sri Lanka, after a five-month break since the World Cup. Despite the political environment being more assured than during the World Cup, Australia still struggled to defeat the Sri Lankans, now full of confidence. Australia overpowered Zimbabwe, before going down the home side. They regrouped and defeated India; however, Sri Lanka defeated Australia, this time in the final. Ponting scored: 53, 46 not out, 0 and 17 for the series.

With Boon's retirement, Ponting was elevated to the No. 3 position in the Test team, and his first assignment in his new role came in a one-off Test against India at the Feroz Shah Kotla in Delhi. Foreshadowing his future Test struggles in India, Ponting made 13 and 14 in a seven-wicket defeat. His failed to regain his form in the following Titan Cup involving India, South Africa and Australia. After a "scratchy" game against South Africa, Ponting was rested for the next match against India. Nevertheless, he was recalled for the return match against South Africa, making 17. The series ending poorly for Ponting, being bowled for a duck, as India won the finals. The pair of ODI tournaments on the subcontinent yielded Ponting only 168 runs at 28.00 from seven matches.

Ponting continued in the role for the series against the West Indies in 1996–97 in Australia. After two Test matches and three scores under 10, he was replaced by Justin Langer, despite scoring 88 in the First Test. He was out of the team for six months, and missed the remaining three

Tests against the West Indies, the three Tests on the tour to South Africa, both series victories to Australia. Many "experts" thought the decision was unjustifiable. Former Australian coach, Bob Simpson, said: "I really feel that Ricky could have been persevered with. He's a fine young cricketer and he'll now have to prove that he's got the tenacity and temperament to go with it." Ponting's axing meant he had time to regain his form in the Sheffield Shield. Despite struggling at first, he scored twin centuries against South Australia in Hobart, and proceeded to score another ton against Queensland.

Ponting was selected for the 1997 Ashes tour of England, but did not play in any of the three preceding ODIs. He was not selected for the first three Tests; England won the first, Australia the third, and the second was drawn. Ponting was given three one-dayers and First-class match against Glamorgan to try to push his case for a Test inclusion. He scored a century in the latter, but managed just five against Middlesex in the last match before the Fourth Test. Michael Bevan was eventually dropped for Ponting, due to poor form and troubles against the short ball.In his first Ashes Test, Ponting scored his first Test century (127, batting at No. 6). He played the last three Tests and ended the series with 241 runs at 48.20.At the time Australia had a policy of the selecting the same team for ODIs, so Ponting only played in three ODIs in early stages of the 1996–97 season in Australia, scoring 68 runs at 22.66 in December 1996 before being dropped.

Ponting scored 119 runs at 39.66 in the three-Test home series against New Zealand in 1997–98, including a breezy 73 not out from 85 balls in the second innings of the First Test in Brisbane to help Australia set a winning target. He then made his first Test century on Australian soil, scoring 105 in the First Test against South Africa at the MCG. He added a fifty in the next match and ended the series with 248 runs at 49.60. Ponting has his most successful ODI season to date, scoring 462 runs at 57.75 in the annual tri-series, including a 100 against New Zealand and three fifties. The 100 was Ponting's third ODI century, but Australia had lost all three matches. He scored 76 in the third and deciding final against South Africa, which Australia won. In a brief four-match ODI tour of New Zealand at the end of the season, Ponting scored 76 runs at 25.33.

 • *1998 tours of the subcontinent and Ashes*

Just 10 days after their tour of New Zealand, Australia played in a first-class warm-up match in India, ahead of their three match Test series. Sachin

Tendulkar struck a double century in the opening warm-up match as the Australian bowlers struggled to cope with the conditions. Ponting came into the Test series with first-class scores of 53, 37 and 155 behind him. Batting at five and seven in the batting order respectively, he scored 18 in the first innings and two in the second on a "dusty turning track" in the opening Test in Chennai. Despite conceding a 71 first innings lead, Tendulkar struck 155 in India's second innings, as India won by 169 runs. Australia suffered further humiliation in the second Test at Eden Gardens. India—whom amassed 5/633 in reply to Australia's 233—went onto win by an innings and 16 runs, as Ponting scored 60 and nine.

Several days after the match, Ponting was thrown out of Equinox night club in Kolkata. The Indian media reported that Ponting was misbehaving with several women in the nightclub. Ponting was fined $1000 by Australian team management for the incident, and later apologised to staff. Ponting later wrote:

A few of the players wanted to go to a nightspot and so this guy had organised for us to get into a nightclub in Calcutta that was usually restricted to members and special guests. When we arrived at the nightclub this same guy spoke to the doorman. He explained that we were Australian cricketers and after a few minutes, they let us in. What we didn't know was that it was a couples night which meant the only way men could get in was in the company of a female. We were quite happy just hanging out together and having a few drinks, and for me it was a chance to celebrate North Melbourne's win in the AFL Ansett Cup final in Melbourne. Everyone was having a good time and knocking down a few beers and the next thing I knew I was asked to leave by one of the security guys. I am usually the last one to leave a nightclub and I wanted to stay, and there was a scuffle but that is all there was to it. I didn't realise we were the only single guys there. To be honest I couldn't remember half of what went on during the night because I'd had a skinful but I definitely did not assault women in the nightclub. Thankfully I had enough witnesses to prove it.

In the following Test in Bangalore, Australia won their first Test in India for 29 years, despite 177 not out from Tendulkar, which gave India a slender first innings lead. Ponting scored 16 his only innings as Australia won by eight wickets. He finished the series with 105 runs at 21.00 as the hosts took the Tests 2–1.

Despite a poor Test series, Ponting's form in ODIs remained strong. In consecutive tournaments in India and Sharjah following the Tests, Ponting scored 467 runs at 51.88. In addition to three fifties, Ponting scored 145 from 158 balls in the Pepsi Cup against Zimbabwe in Delhi, equalling Dean Jones' Australian record.

Ponting also had his first confrontation with Harbhajan Singh, an Indian off spinner who went on to have much success against him. In the Coca-Cola Cup series ODI against India in April, he and Mark Waugh put on more than 80 runs in 12 overs before Harbhajan was introduced into the attack. In the spinners second over, Ponting took him for four then lofted him over mid-wicket for six next ball. The following delivery saw Ponting use his feet in an attempt to get to the pitch of the ball but missed the shot and was consequently stumped. After the dismissal the pair clashed verbally. Ponting wrote, "The Sharjah incident was the result of me being over-competitive but it had the potential to get quite nasty.

I was really disappointed with the shot I played [to get dismissed] and when I looked up Harbahjan was right in my face giving me the finger [gesturing for Ponting to leave the ground with his index finger] and really mouthing off. Had he been a few more metres away from me I would have not reacted like I did or at the most I would have given him a bit of lip as I walked past. I just over-reacted to the provocation." Both players were consequently fined ($500) and reprimanded by the match referee, with Harbhajan also suspended for a single ODI as he was adjudged to have breached the ICC Cricket Code of Conduct.

On the subsequent tour of Pakistan less than six months later, Ponting was dropped in favour of Darren Lehmann. The left-hander was perceived to be a better player of spin and a better prospect on the dry pitches of the Indian subcontinent than Ponting. In the first Test starting in October, Lehmann scored 98 in Rawalpindi, as Australia won their first Test in Pakistan in 39 years. Ponting's only Test outing was in a high-scoring second Test draw in Peshawar, when he scored 76 not out and 43 as Lehmann was injured. The match saw Mark Taylor equal Don Bradman's Australian record score of 334, when he declared Australia's innings overnight on 4/599, despite being not out. Ponting was replaced by Lehmann for the final Test.

In between the Tests and the ODIs, Australia were knocked out of the 1998 Wills International Cup, starting in late October, when they were defeated by India in their opening match. In a knockout based tournament, Tendulkar scored 141 in India's total of 307; meanwhile, Ponting managed a 53 ball 41, in a 44 run defeat. In a tournament hosted in Bangladesh, South

Africa were eventual victors, defeating the West Indies in the final. He played in all the following ODIs against Pakistan, which Australia won 3–0. In the final match, Ponting scored 124 not out from 129 balls, as Australia chased down 316 with six wickets to spare. He finished the series with 215 runs at 107.50.

When the Australians returned for the home series against England, Ponting was "in the worst run-scoring groove in his first-class career." Nevertheless, he was recalled in place of Lehmann, despite the latter's form in Pakistan. This was explained on the basis of "horses for courses"; it was reasoned that Ponting would be more effective against England's pace-oriented bowling attack.

However, Ponting struggled in the first three Tests, scoring 47 runs at 11.75, and Lehmann regained his spot for the last two matches. He had played 22 Tests by the end of 1998, with 1,209 runs at an average of 36.63. Ponting was a permanent fixture in the ODI team throughout this period, and scored 322 runs at 46.00 during the Carlton & United (CUB series) series of 1998–99. During the CUB series, Ponting was involved in a fight outside a pub in Kings Cross, New South Wales, and earned a three match suspension from the national team. He sustained a black eye in the fight. Forced to front a media conference with the black eye, Ponting admitted that he had a "problem with alcohol,"and sought external help to attend to this problem. He also thought that his career was on "thin ice" and he had "overstepped" the mark, along with admitting that the episode may have ended his International captaincy aspirations.

- *1999–2002 The road back to the Australian side*

Mark Taylor retired from international cricket on 2 February 1999, and was replaced by ODI captain Steve Waugh. Lehmann failed to make much impact in the final two Ashes Tests and was dropped for the 1998–99 tour of the West Indies, while Ponting was recalled. Ponting's ability against pace-bowling helped his push for inclusion, as the West Indies typically relied entirely on pacemen. However, he was unable to force his way into the side in the first two tests, with number three, Justin Langer, and number six, Greg Blewett, cementing their places in the side.

Before the third Test, Blewett suffered a hand injury and Ponting was recalled into the side. On a pitch that became increasingly flat throughout the day, Ponting—who came to the crease with the score at 4–144—joined

Steve Waugh in a 281 partnership. After Waugh survived one of Ambrose's "more threatening spells", he scored 199 and Ponting 104. He "batted with maturity and even temperament associated with the champions of the game", according to Waugh. Australia collapsed in their second innings to be bowled out for 146, with Ponting scoring 22.Left with a record run-chase in Barbados, the West Indies won by a single wicket, thanks to an unbeaten Brian Lara century. Australia had to win the Fourth and final Test in Antigua to retain the series, after going down 2–1. Ponting scored 21 and 21 not out in the match, as Australia won by 176 runs. The following seven-match ODI series was not a success for Ponting, scoring just 74 runs at 14.80 in five matches. The series was drawn at 3-all and included a tie.

- *First World Cup success (1999)*

Australia started their 1999 World Cup campaign in England with success against minnows Scotland, before defeats by Pakistan and New Zealand. Ponting scored, 33, 47 and 49 respectively. After the twin defeats, pundits doubted whether Australia could make the semi-finals let alone win the tournament. Australia then defeated Bangladesh with 30 overs to spare, as Ponting batted out of his usual number three spot for the only time in the tournament. In an attempt to increase the run-rate with pinch hitter Brendon Julian, Ponting scored an unbeaten 18 from 10 balls at number four.

Ponting scored 20, 23 and 36 in the following matches against the West Indies, India and Zimbabwe. In the last match of the Super Six stage of the tournament, Australia were to play South Africa in a match they needed to win to make the semi-finals. South Africa batted first and scored 271, before Australia slumped to 3/48. Steve Waugh joined Ponting in the middle and scored 22 runs in ten overs. Both then agreed increase the scoring in a mid-pitch conversation. South African all-rounder Jacques Kallis could not bowl because of strained abdominal muscles and the batting pair attacked the replacement bowlers, scoring 82 from 10 overs. They were involved in a 126-run stand until Ponting fell for 69 scored in 110 balls, including five fours and two sixes. Waugh went on to make 120 off 110 deliveries helping Australia win with two balls to spare.

The sides met again in their next match, this time in the semi-final at Edgbaston on 17 June 1999. Australia only managed 213, with Ponting contributing a solid 37 from 48 balls. In reply, South Africa started strongly, talking 45 from the first nine overs without the loss of a wicket. However, Warne dismissed Herschelle Gibbs and Gary Kirsten before long and eventually took 4/29 from 10 overs. The last over started with the Africans needing nine runs with one wicket in hand. Lower-order hitter, Lance Klusener, proceeded to score eight runs in the next two balls. Drama followed, as Donald was run-out two balls later, resulting in a tie. Australia qualified for the final because they finished higher than their opposition on the Super Six table. They comfortably accounted for Pakistan in the final, winning by eight wickets, after they were set a target of 132. Ponting scored 24 in Australia's first World Cup win since 1987. He ended the tournament with 354 runs at 39.33.

Australia soon travelled to Sri Lanka for a three-Test series, which they lost 1–0. Ponting was one of Australia's few effective players during the tour and was Man-of-the-Series, ending with 253 runs at 84.33. In the First Test defeat at Kandy, Ponting scored 96 and 51, almost half of Australia's match total of 328 runs. They lost the match by six wickets, partly due to being unable to handle the spin of Muralitharan who took eight wickets. The Second Test was severely interrupted by rain and Ponting scored just one in his only innings. He scored 105 not out in the Third Test in Colombo, his only Test century in Sri Lanka. Despite having a perceived weakness against spin, Ponting played Muralitharan the best out of all the Australian batsmen.

He scored 31 as Australia won their inaugural Test against Zimbabwe by nine wickets. In the following ODI series between the respective countries, Ponting scored 288 runs at 57.60 with two fifties.

Ponting started the 1999–2000 season poorly, with ducks in his first three Test innings in the series against Pakistan, including a pair on his home ground Bellerive Oval. He ended the run in style, scoring 197 in the Third Test at the WACA. Australia won the series 3–0 and Ponting proceeded to score 125 in the First Test against India at the Adelaide Oval. He finished with an unbeaten 141 in the Third Test at the SCG, the culmination of another Australian whitewash.

Ponting was the leading scorer for the series, compiling 375 runs at 125.00. He brought this form into the initial stages of the following 1999–2000 Carlton United ODI series, hitting 32 and 115, before three consecutive ducks. Ponting, however, ended the rut towards the back end of the series, stringing together 53, 43, 33, 50 and 78, as Australia won the tournament. Along with his impressive average of 40.4, Ponting's strike rate (87.06) was the highest of all recognised Australian batsmen. Perhaps more importantly, Ponting was selected as temporary vice-captain when Shane Warne was unavailable through injury, strengthening his claim for future higher honours. "It's now apparent to me that I'm one being viewed as a future Australia captain", Ponting acknowledged in his newspaper column. "I think it's fair to say unless I was being considered for a future leadership position in the team then someone with significantly more experience, like Mark [Waugh] would have been given the nod to be the team's vice-captain.

Despite all his good fortune, Ponting slid into the boundary fence and seriously damaged his ankle during the second final against Pakistan, forcing him to miss the upcoming ODI series' in New Zealand and South Africa. The damaged ligaments required a two-hour operation, with doctors telling him how he would not be able to return to cricket until the next summer. He recovered quicker than expected and by May he returned to the golf course and was given approval to start cricket training. He returned to the international scene in August for a three-match ODI series against South Africa in Melbourne's indoor Docklands Stadium. He made only 60 runs, as the series was tied 1–1, with a tie.

Ahead of the first Test of the 2000–01 season in November, Ponting found form while playing for Tasmania. He scored 233 against a strong Queensland bowling team that included Andy Bichel, Adam Dale and Ashley Noffke. The innings included 37 boundaries and four sixes, and was so dominant, the next highest score for the innings was 61. In the second and final first-class match Ponting played for Tasmania in the season, he scored a more sedate 187 against New South Wales in Hobart, assuring him a place in the Test side, despite Damien Martyn (who replaced Ponting in the side when injured) scoring two centuries for Western Australia.

Ponting was overlooked the ODI vice-captaincy, with Gilchrist given the role; however, Ponting captained a Northern Territory XI against the West Indies in the lead-up to the upcoming series. Though not known for extravagant claims, Steve Waugh told a journalist that Ponting could easily be the best batsman in the world, and put him alongside Sachin Tendulkar and Brian Lara. When Jamie Cox was selected for Australia A, Ponting was selected as captain of Tasmania for a domestic one-dayer against Victoria in December. His men won by nine wickets, with Ponting scoring an unbeaten 64 from 69 balls. Australia white-washed the West Indies 5–0 in the Test series; Ponting scored a modest 242 runs at 40.33, with a high score of 92.

• *Defeat in India and 2001 Ashes*

Injury aside (he missed a three-Test tour of New Zealand in early 2000 after hurting his ankle in a fielding mishap in an ODI Final at Sydney), his position was now secured. Australia toured India in between February and April for three Tests and five ODIs. Australia had not won a Test series in India since 1969. Australian captain Steve Waugh began calling this the "Final Frontier". Australia lost the series 2–1 after winning the first Test, and Ponting finished with just 17 runs at an average of 3.4. He was dismissed all five times by Harbhajan Singh. Ponting had a habit of instinctively rocking onto the front foot and thrusting his wrists at Harbhajan's deliveries and was frequently caught in the bat pad positions because of this.

Despite this recent run of poor scores, Ponting was promoted to the key No. 3 position in the Australian batting order at the expense of the dropped Justin Langer, while Damien Martyn took Ponting's former spot at No. 6, for the very next Test series, the 2001 Ashes tour of England. Ponting began the series poorly, scoring 11, 14, 4, 14 and 17—the first four dismissals all to Darren Gough. In the first innings of the fourth Test, Ponting stood his ground while on 0 after edging to slips and refused to go off the field without a TV replay. Replays revealed that the ball had been grassed and Ponting subsequently went on to score 144 and 72 in the second innings. He scored his 216 runs in only 226 balls. In doing so, he repeated his feat in 1997 of returning to form at Headingley. He ended the series with 338 runs at 42.25. Starting with that 2001 Ashes series he has batted No. 3 in all but four of his Test innings.

The touring New Zealanders were not expected to provide much of a challenge to the in-form Australians during the three-match Test series starting in November. The opening Test in Brisbane, saw the tourists came within 11 runs of victory, before the Test was drawn; partly to do with inclement weather. Ponting scored five and a run-a-ball 32 not out in Australia's second innings, as they pushed for a declaration. After scoring 4, 0 and 0 in his previous Test outings at Bellerive Oval, Ponting broke through with a man-of-the-match performance of 157 not out in the Second Test, before further rain resulted in another draw. The result of the Third Test in Perth was no different, with Ponting scoring 31 and 26. Set a record 440 to win, Australia finished on 7/381 at stumps on the final day, despite half-centuries from Gilchrist and the Waugh twins. He ended the Test season 366 runs at 52.28.

> • *2002–2004: Appointment as One Day International captain*

Appointment as One Day International captain Ponting at a training session at the Adelaide Oval in 2009.

Although the Test team had continued to perform well, sweeping South Africa 3–0 in the home series in 2001–02, the One-Day International (ODI) team suffered a slump, failing to qualify for the finals of the triangular tournament, leading to the dropping of Steve Waugh from the one-day team in February 2002. Ponting was elevated to the captaincy, ahead of then vice-captain Adam Gilchrist. The fortunes of the ODI team revived immediately, and Ponting's men won their first series during the tour of South Africa, defeating the team that had won the tournament which ended Waugh's reign.

Following his elevation to the ODI captaincy, Ponting played a prominent role in the Test tour of South Africa. He scored 100 not out to steer Australia to a four-wicket win in the Second Test in Cape Town, bringing up the winning runs with a six from the bowling of Paul Adams. He struck 89 in the Third Test and ended the series with 308 runs at 77.25 with a strike rate of 76.48. Australia entered the seven-match ODI series without both of the Waugh twins.

Ponting was prominent in the 3–0 whitewash of Pakistan on neutral territory in late 2002. He struck 141 in the First Test in Colombo and 150 in the Third Test in Sharjah to end with 342 runs at 85.50.

> • *2002–03 Ashes victory and first World Cup success as captain*

England toured for the 2002–03 Australian season, and Ponting struck 123 in the First Test in Brisbane. His form continued with 154 in the Second Test in Adelaide, meaning that he had scored four centuries in five Tests. Australia won the latter match by an innings and Ponting scored 68 in the Third Test in Perth as Australia took an unassailable 3–0 lead. He was unable to pass fifty in the final two Tests and ended the series with 417 runs at 52.12.

Australia won the VB series held between and after the Tests. After the conclusion of the Third Test, Australia's 30-man squad for upcoming 2003 World Cup was announced. Steve Waugh was a somewhat surprising omission, despite being unable to force his way back into the ODI team since being dropped after team disappointment in the 2001–02 VB Series

Ponting scored a slow 18 from 30 deliveries in Australia's victory in the opening match of the 2002–03 VB series against England in Sydney. He proceeded to score 119 from 123 balls (nine fours and three sixes) in Australia's second match of the series—again against England, this time at the MCG—sharing an all wicket record Australian ODI partnership of 225 with Adam Gilchrist in the process. Despite a comfortable Australian victory, Warne dislocated his right shoulder while diving to stop a ball. The success continued through the 2002–03 ODI series in Australia. Winning the finals series against England 2–0.

Australia hit trouble on the personnel front in the lead up to the World Cup. Lehmann was handed a seven-match ban for racial abuse, the world's number 1 ranked ODI batsman Michael Bevan was injured, as was all rounder Shane Watson, who had to withdraw from the World Cup. At the time, another all-rounder, Andrew Symonds, had been performing poorly and had been heavily maligned by cricket analysts, but Ponting strongly advocated his inclusion. The selectors granted Ponting his wish, although the decision was considered highly controversial, especially with Waugh campaigning for his recall as an all-rounder.

A few days before the tournament started, Australia were in further turmoil, when leading bowler Shane Warne was sent home after failing a drugs test, and a replacement could not be flown in until after the first match. With Bevan and Lehmann still sidelined, Australia went into their opening match with little choice over their line-up, and Symonds having to play. However, Symonds repaid Ponting's faith with an unbeaten 140 after Australia lost three quick wickets to be in early trouble. Australia beat Pakistan, and gained further momentum by defeating India by nine wickets in less than half their allotted overs in the next match. Symonds continued to put in a series of match-winning performances and continued to be strongly backed by Ponting from then on. Ponting himself performed solidly with 53 against Pakistan and 24 not out, hitting the winning runs to guide Australia home.

He failed to perform in the rest of the group matches including just 2 against Namibia and 18 against England in a poor performance which Australia managed to win just. He began the Super Six stage with a massive 114 against Sri Lanka. This innings included 4 sixes and he was very aggressive. He failed in the rest of the Super Six stage and the semi-final against the same opposition (Sri Lanka). In the Final, they met India, who they had crushed in the group stage. Indian captain Sourav Ganguly controversially sent the Australians in to bat, citing cloud cover, but Ponting's batsmen attacked immediately and put the Indian bowlers under pressure. They went on to score 359–2, a record for a world cup final by over 100 runs. Ponting top-scored with a brilliant 140 not out from 121 balls. India's batsmen could not cope with the target, and were defeated by a record (for World Cup Final matches) 125 runs.

"I have had some amazing times and some proud moments in my career, but the events at the Wanderers have topped the lot. Lifting the World Cup alongside 20 other proud Australians ... [It is] without doubt the best moment of my cricketing life."Ponting led his team to a dominant, undefeated, performance in the 2003 Cricket World Cup, winning all 11 of their matches.

Ponting was announced as long-term vice-captain in place of Adam Gilchrist for Australia's away series in the Caribbean starting in April 2003. The first Test was not the first time Ponting had been vice-captain of the Australian Test team however, as he was thrust into the role against the West Indies in 2000 and England in 2001—because of injuries to Steve Waugh. Although Gilchrist had not done anything untoward, Ponting was elevated because Australian selectors wanted him to captain if Waugh was to be injured. This was Ponting's third tour to the Caribbean, and he was rested from the only warm-up match ahead of the Tests.

Nevertheless, he continued his World Cup form in the First Test, scoring 117 and 42 not out on a slow and low pitch, as Australia won by nine wickets. Ponting scored his first double century (206) in the Second Test, as he and Darren Lehmann shared an Australian third-wicket partnership record of 315 against a weak bowling attack. Australia defeated the West Indies by 118 runs on the final day—retaining the Frank Worrell Trophy.The Tasmanian's rich vein of form continued in the Third Test, after being rested for a tour match against Barbados. He scored 113 before running himself out, as Australia batted first on a pitch at the Kensington Oval described as the slowest Waugh had played on. Waugh's men proceeded to take a 3–0 series, with a comfortable nine-wicket victory. Ponting missed the final Test, as Australia conceded the Test record run chase of 418; nevertheless, Ponting was still awarded the man-of-the-series award, after ending the series with 523 runs at 130.75.

- *5,000 Test runs*

Ponting then scored 10 and 59 as Australia recorded comfortable innings victories in their inaugural series against Bangladesh, played in Darwin and Cairns in the tropical north of Australia in the winter of 2003. In the third and final match of the ODI series following the Tests, Ponting scored a composed century, as he and Michael Bevan put on a run-a-ball 127-run stand.

Australia's cricket summer started in October; a month earlier than usual because of their ODI series in India following their home series against Zimbabwe. Due to the season's early start, many of the Australian players were not match fit. McGrath missed the series with an ankle injury, while there were concerns about whether Australia should be playing Zimbabwe because of Robert Mugabe's regime. The first Test started on 9 October in Perth, as Australia started strongly batted first against a Zimbabwean bowling attack that lacked penetration on a flat WACA wicket.

However, Ponting was dismissed leg before wicket for 37, while Hayden went on to break Brian Lara's world record Test score of 375.Australia won the Test by an innings and 175 runs on the final day. In the next Test at the SCG Australia fielded an inexperienced team due to injuries and won by nine wickets; sweeping the series 2–0. Ponting struck 169 and 53 not out, and passed 5,000 Test runs during his first innings century. The Australian number three ended the two-match series with 259 runs at 129.50. In the midst of the lack of public attention and poor crowds, Ponting wrote how he was unsure whether Bangladesh and Zimbabwe should be playing Test cricket.

Australia flew to India two-day after the conclusion of the Zimbabwean series to play in the TVS Cup against India and New Zealand. They opened their campaign on 26 October against India in Gwalior, but were defeated by 37 runs, as Ponting was dismissed for two. Australia played New Zealand in match three of series in Faridabad. An early 9 AM start saw New Zealand bowled out for 97, despite Australia bowling 17 wides. Australia comfortably reached the target, losing only two wickets in the process; one of which was Ponting for 12, who felt that he was "in terrible form.".

Before Australia's next game, Ponting was named the Wisden International Cricketer of the Year in an award ceremony in Mumbai. Two days later, the city saw Australia defeat India by 77 runs, helped by Ponting's 31. He continued his run without a large score, managing just 16 in the fifth match of the series against New Zealand; however, Australia won a hard-fought contest.

He regained his form in a victory over New Zealand in match—scoring 52 in Guwahati. Ponting improved further against India in match eight in Bangalore. After Gilchrist scored his first ODI century against India, Ponting scored an unbeaten 108 from 103 balls, to help Australia win by 61 runs. Ponting hit seven sixes and one four, becoming the first batsman to end up with only one four in an ODI century. Ponting struggled to come to terms with the pitch early, reaching his 50 in 69 balls, before scoring his next 50 in 31 deliveries. After defeating New Zealand, India qualified for the final against Australia. Batting first in Kolkata, Australia managed 5/235, as Ponting scored 36. India were bowled out for 198, leaving Australia victors by 37 runs. He finished the series with 296 runs—the third highest run-scorer—at an average of 42.83.

- *Most runs by an Australian in a calendar year (2003)*

After making 54 and 50 in the rain-drawn First Test in Brisbane, Ponting scored double-centuries in back-to-back Tests against India, in the Second Test at Adelaide (242) and at Melbourne (257, his career high). He hit 31 not out in the second innings in Melbourne as Australia levelled the series 1–1 and scored 25 and 47 in the drawn Fourth Test in Sydney to end as the leading run-scorer for the series, with 706 runs at 100.85. Harbhajan had been sent home after the First Test with an injury to his spinning finger.

Having also scored 206 at Port-of-Spain earlier in the year, he became only the second player (Sir Donald Bradman the other) to hit three double-centuries in a calendar year. Ponting's 242 against India at Adelaide is also the highest ever Test score by a batsman whose team was subsequently defeated in the match. After Steve Waugh's retirement at the beginning of 2004 following the drawn home series against India, Ponting assumed the Test captaincy. Since 1997 the Australian team has not always had the same captain for Tests and for ODIs, with Mark Taylor and Steve Waugh being dropped from the ODI team whilst still the Test captain.

2011–2012: Post-captaincy

- *2010–11 Ashes defeat*

Australia entered the 2010–11 Ashes series hoping to regain The Ashes from England on home soil as they had four years previously. The First Test in Brisbane was drawn after both sides posted large batting totals. Ponting was caught behind for 10 in the first innings and 51 not out in the second. A barren run followed in the subsequent three Tests, scoring 52 runs in total as Australia lost the series. Ponting became the first Australian captain to lose an Ashes series in Australia since Allan Border in 1987. During the Fourth Test Ponting was involved in an on-field argument with umpires, and was fined 40% of his match fee, which accounted to around $5,400.

Ponting missed the Fifth Test due to a finger injury, and Michael Clarke stood in as Australia's captain. Australia's heavy defeat in the series and Ponting's poor run of form caused his position in the team to be questioned. Former Australian captain Steve Waugh suggested dropping him down the batting order others, such as former Australian batsman and South African captain Kepler Wessels, called for him to relinquish the captaincy to focus on his batting.Yet, for his performances in 2010, he was named as captain of the World ODI XI by the ICC.

- 2011 World Cup and resignation as captain

Ponting retained the captaincy of Australia for the 2011 World Cup in India, Sri Lanka and Bangladesh. Australia had won the previous three World Cups and entered the tournament as the world's top-ranked ODI team. Australia qualified for the quarter-finals, although Ponting failed to find form, scoring 102 runs in five innings during the group stage of the tournament. Australia met India in the quarter-finals and were defeated by five wickets. Ponting scored 104,his first century in international cricket in over a year. After being knocked out of the tournament, Ponting resigned his position as captain at both Test and ODI levels, endorsed Michael Clarke as his successor, and indicated his intention to continue playing.

- *2011–2012: Post-captaincy*

In 2011, Ponting was inducted into Australian Institute of Sport (AIS) 'Best of the Best'.He was selected in Michael Clarke's teams for the tours of Sri Lanka and South Africa in 2011, scoring an important half-century (62) in the fourth innings of the second Test against South Africa in Johannesburg, helping Australia chase down a target of 310 to draw the series 1–1.

In the 2011–12 Australian summer, a disappointing series draw with New Zealand gave rise to calls for Ponting to be removed from the team following perceived underperformances. The selectors resisted the calls, selecting Ponting for the Boxing Day Test—the first of a four-Test series against India.

Ponting scored two half-centuries in Australia's first Test win, followed by a century (134) in Australia's first innings of the second Test in Sydney. The century was his first in Test cricket in almost two years. His fourth-wicket partnership of 288 runs with Clarke, who went on to make 329 not out, set a new record for the biggest partnership by an Australian pair of batsmen against India.Australia sealed the series win by defeating India in Perth, and in the fourth Test in Adelaide, Ponting and Clarke beat their own record, putting on 386 runs. The partnership was the fourth highest to that point in Australian Test cricket. Ponting's own score was 221. During the innings, he became only the third player and the first Australian (after Sachin Tendulkar and Rahul Dravid, who were playing in the same match) to pass 13,000 career Test runs.

- *2012: Test retirement*

On Australia Day 2012 he was appointed as an Officer of the Order of Australia for services to cricket and, through the Ponting Foundation, the community. Ponting was promoted to captain in the 2011–12 Commonwealth Bank Series in Australia in Michael Clarke's absence due to injury. However, after only two games as captain he was dropped, having scored only 18 runs in 5 games of the 2011–12 Commonwealth Bank Series. At a press conference thereafter, Ponting conceded, "I don't expect to play one-day international cricket for Australia any more and I'm pretty sure the selectors don't expect to pick me either ... I will continue playing Test cricket and I'll continue playing for Tasmania as well".

On 29 November 2012 Ponting announced that he would retire from Test cricket after the WACA test against South Africa.

- *2013: Tasmania and Surrey*

After retiring from test cricket, Ponting played out the Sheffield Shield season with eventual champions Tasmania. He was the competition's leading run scorer with 911 runs at an average of 75.91. As a result of his prolific form with the bat, he was named the Sheffield Shield player of the year.

He signed on to play for the English County side Surrey during June–July 2013. His score of 192 on debut against Derbyshire was the highest score by a Surrey batsman on their first class debut for the county. Ponting scored an unbeaten 169 against Nottinghamshire in his final first class innings, ensuring his team held on for a draw.

- *During the Ashes 2013, Ponting wrote a regular column for the Daily Mail*

At the formal opening of the Bellerive Oval redevelopment in January 2015, it was announced that the new Western Stand would be named the Ricky Ponting Stand in his honour.On 9 December 2015 Ponting also unveiled a bronze statue placed at the ground in his honour.

- *Playing style*

Ponting was known as an aggressive competitor, as manifested in his on-field conduct. According to former Australian captain Allan Border, what you see with Ponting is what you get, and "he wears his heart on his sleeve". Border also noted that Ponting has an abundance of determination, courage and skill.

However, his competitive attitudes could be overly aggressive, pushing the boundaries of cricket etiquette. In early 2006, in the Chappell–Hadlee Trophy, Ponting had an on-field argument with umpire Billy Bowden over signalling a no-ball because not enough players were within the inner circle. In mid-2006, during a tour of Bangladesh, Ponting was accused of "badgering the umpires until he got what he wanted".

The South African captain, Graeme Smith, described Ponting as the toughest competitor he had ever played against.

- *List of international cricket centuries by Ricky Ponting*

Ponting was known as an aggressive right-handed batsman who played a wide repertoire of shots with confidence, most notably the pull and hook. However, he had some technical weaknesses, such as shuffling across his stumps and being trapped leg before wicket, and thrusting his bat away from his body—especially early in his innings, because he wants to move forward and across to drive rather than backwards and across to cut the ball.

Despite being widely renowned as the best player of the hook and pull shots in the world, Ponting was equally adept on both the front and back foot. However, during the latter stages of his career, the hook and pull shots have often been the cause of his dismissal.He adopts a more traditional V-grip lower down the handle as he is a short batsman that doesn't have natural power on the shot.

He was considered by some observers to have trouble against quality spin, especially against Indian off spinner Harbhajan Singh, who dismissed Ponting on 13 occasions in international cricket. Ponting had a tendency to rock onto the front foot and thrust his wrists at spinning deliveries, resulting in many catches close to the wicket. Ponting rarely employed the sweep shot against spin, something considered unusual for a top-order batsman. Instead, he looked to use his feet to come down the wicket to spinners, or play off the back foot through the off-side. Former West Indian captain, Viv Richards, who was rated as the third best Test cricketer in a 2002 poll by Wisden, said Ponting was his favourite current-day player to watch, slightly ahead of Sachin Tendulkar.

This is the complete graphical representation of the test cricket record of Ricky Ponting. Individual innings are represented by the blue and red (not out) bars; the green line is his career batting average. Current as of 8 January 2019.

- *Bowling and fielding*

A right-arm medium bowler who tends to bowl off cutters or faster offspin,[303] Ponting rarely bowled, although he has notably dismissed West Indian batsman Brian Lara in an ODI match and former England captain Michael Vaughan in an Ashes Test in 2005. He was also ceremoniously asked to bowl in his final test match against South Africa in 2012. He was, however, rated one of the best fielders in the world. He usually fielded in the slips, cover and silly point. His good eye and accurate throws often saw him run batsmen out with direct hits.

- *Record as captain*

Ponting has often been criticised for his lack of imagination in his captaincy, though many players who played under him say he is a good leader. According to former Australian opening batsman Justin Langer, "He is quite inspirational as a leader and I just never get all the detractors he has. Whether it's in the fielding practice, the nets, the way he holds himself off the field—every time he speaks, these young guys just listen, they hang on every word he says."

"Ponting captained 2 consecutive World Cup victories in 2003 and 2007 (out of Australia's hat-trick of World Cups – 1999, 2003, 2007)"

Records and achievements

• *Records and achievements*

Ponting was the Wisden Leading Cricketer in the World in 2003 and one of the five Wisden Cricketers of the Year for 2006. He has been the Allan Border Medalist a record four times in 2004, 2006, 2007 and 2009 (with Michael Clarke). Ponting has won the award of Australia's best Test player in 2003, 2004 and 2007 and Australia's best One Day International player in 2002 and 2007.

1. First batsman to score centuries in ODI cricket against all Test playing nations (Afghanistan and Ireland were not awarded Test status in Ponting's playing period).
2. Ponting, along with Shane Watson, holds the record for the highest partnership for any wicket in the ICC Champions Trophy (252 not out for the second wicket).
3. Ponting's score of 242 against India is the highest individual Test innings in a losing cause.
4. He was awarded the Allan Border Medal by the CA in 2004, 2006, 2007 and 2009.
5. He was named an Australia Post Legend of Cricket in 2021.

• *Coaching role : Ponting during the 2017-18 Tri-Series*

1. On 1 January 2017, Ponting was named an interim coach for Australia's T20I series against Sri Lanka. Ponting also coached the Mumbai Indians in the IPL from 2014 to 2016. Ponting was appointed as the new coach of Delhi Daredevils (now Delhi Capitals) in the IPL on 3 January 2018.
2. Ponting joined the Australian cricket coaching team as an assistant for the 2017–18 Trans-Tasman Tri-Series.

CHAPTER TWO

Australia national cricket team

- Australia national cricket team

The Australia men's national cricket team represents Australia in men's international cricket. As the joint oldest team in Test cricket history, playing in the first ever Test match in 1877, the team also plays One-Day International (ODI) and Twenty20 International (T20I) cricket, participating in both the first ODI, against England in the 1970–71 season and the first T20I, against New Zealand in the 2004–05 season, winning both games. The team draws its players from teams playing in the Australian domestic competitions – the Sheffield Shield, the Australian domestic limited-overs cricket tournament and the Big Bash League.

The national team has played 837 Test matches, winning 397, losing 226, drawing 212 and tying 2. As of January 2021, Australia is ranked third in the ICC Test Championship on 113 rating points. Australia is the most successful team in Test cricket history, in terms of overall wins, win-loss ratio and wins percentage.

Test rivalries include The Ashes (with England), The Border-Gavaskar Trophy (with India), the Frank Worrell Trophy (with the West Indies), the Trans-Tasman Trophy (with New Zealand), and with South Africa.

The team has played 958 ODI matches, winning 581, losing 334, tying 9 and with 34 ending in a no-result. As of January 2021, Australia is ranked fourth in the ICC ODI Championship on 111 rating points, though have been ranked first for 141 of 185 months since its introduction in 2002.

Australia is the most successful team in ODI cricket history, winning more than 60 per cent of their matches, with a record seven World Cup final appearances (1975, 1987, 1996, 1999, 2003, 2007 and 2015) and have won the World Cup a record five times: 1987, 1999, 2003, 2007 and 2015. Australia is the first (and only) team to appear in four consecutive World Cup finals (1996, 1999, 2003 and 2007), surpassing the old record of three consecutive World Cup appearances by the West Indies (1975, 1979 and 1983) and the first and only team to win 3 consecutive World Cups (1999, 2003 and 2007). The team was undefeated in 34 consecutive World Cup matches until the 2011 Cricket World Cup where Pakistan beat them by 4 wickets in the Group stage.

It is also the second team to win a World Cup (2015) on home soil, after India (2011). Australia have also won the ICC Champions Trophy twice (2006 and 2009) making them the first and the only team to become back to back winners in the Champions Trophy tournaments. As of 2021, Australia is the only team to win five Cricket World Cups; no other team has won more than two.

The national team has played 153 Twenty20 International matches, winning 79, losing 69, tying 2 and with 3 ending in a no-result. As of November 2021, Australia is ranked sixth in the ICC T20I Championship on 246 rating points. Australia are the reigning ICC Men's T20 World Cup champions, defeating New Zealand in the 2021 final to claim their first T20 World Cup title.

On 12 January 2019, Australia won the first ODI against India at the Sydney Cricket Ground by 34 runs, to record their 1,000[th] win in international cricket.

- Australian cricket from 1876–77 to 1890

The Australian team that toured England in 1878
The Australian cricket team participated in the first Test match at the MCG in 1877, defeating an English team by 45 runs, with Charles Bannerman making the first Test century, a score of 165 retired hurt.Test cricket, which only occurred between Australia and England at the time, was limited by the long distance between the two countries, which would take several months by sea. Despite Australia's much smaller population, the team was very competitive in early games, producing stars such as Jack Blackham, Billy Murdoch, Fred "The Demon" Spofforth, George Bonnor, Percy McDonnell, George Giffen and Charles "The Terror" Turner. Most cricketers at the time were either from New South Wales or Victoria, with

the notable exception of George Giffen, the star South Australian all-rounder.

A highlight of Australia's early history was the 1882 Test match against England at The Oval. In this match, Fred Spofforth took 7/44 in the game's fourth innings to save the match by preventing England from making their 85-run target. After this match The Sporting Times, a major newspaper in London at the time, printed a mock obituary in which the death of English cricket was proclaimed and the announcement made that "the body was cremated and the ashes taken to Australia." This was the start of the famous Ashes series in which Australia and England play a series of Test matches to decide the holder of the Ashes. To this day, the contest is one of the fiercest rivalries in sport.

- Golden age

History of Australian cricket from 1890–91 to 1900 and History of Australian cricket from 1900–01 to 1918

The so-called 'Golden Age' of Australian Test cricket occurred around the end of the 19th century and the beginning of the 20th century, with the team under the captaincy of Joe Darling, Monty Noble and Clem Hill winning eight of ten tours. It is considered to have lasted from the 1897–98 English tour of Australia and the 1910–11 South African tour of Australia. Outstanding batsmen such as Joe Darling, Clem Hill, Reggie Duff, Syd Gregory, Warren Bardsley and Victor Trumper, brilliant all-rounders including Monty Noble, George Giffen, Harry Trott and Warwick Armstrong and excellent bowlers including Ernie Jones, Hugh Trumble, Tibby Cotter, Bill Howell, Jack Saunders and Bill Whitty, all helped Australia to become the dominant cricketing nation for most of this period.

Victor Trumper became one of Australia's first sporting heroes, and was widely considered Australia's greatest batsman before Bradman and one of the most popular players. He played a record (at the time) number of Tests at 49 and scored 3163 (another record) runs at a high for the time average of 39.04. His early death in 1915 at the age of 37 from kidney disease caused national mourning. The Wisden Cricketers' Almanack, in its obituary for him, called him Australia's greatest batsman: "Of all the great Australian batsmen Victor Trumper was by general consent the best and most brilliant."

The years leading up to the start of World War I were marred by conflict between the players, led by Clem Hill, Victor Trumper and Frank Laver, the Australian Board of Control for International Cricket, led by Peter McAlister, who was attempting to gain more control of tours from the players. This led to six leading players (the so-called "Big Six") walking out on the 1912 Triangular Tournament in England, with Australia fielding what was generally considered a second-rate side. This was the last series before the war, and no more cricket was played by Australia for eight years, with Tibby Cotter being killed in Palestine during the war.

• Australian cricket from 1918–19 to 1930

Test cricket resumed in the 1920/21 season in Australia with a touring English team, captained by Johnny Douglas losing all five Tests to Australia, captained by the "Big Ship" Warwick Armstrong. Several players from before the war, including Warwick Armstrong, Charlie Macartney, Charles Kelleway, Warren Bardsley and the wicket-keeper Sammy Carter, were instrumental in the team's success, as well as new players Herbie Collins, Jack Ryder, Bert Oldfield, the spinner Arthur Mailey and the so-called "twin destroyers" Jack Gregory and Ted McDonald. The team continued its success on the 1921 tour of England, winning three out of the five Tests in Warwick Armstrong's last series. The side was, on the whole, inconsistent in the latter half of the 1920s, losing its first home Ashes series since the 1911–12 season in 1928–29.

• Australian cricket from 1930–31 to 1945

The 1930 tour of England heralded a new age of success for the Australian team. The team, led by Bill Woodfull – the "Great Un-bowlable" – featured legends of the game including Bill Ponsford, Stan McCabe, Clarrie Grimmett and the young pair of Archie Jackson and Don Bradman. Bradman was the outstanding batsman of the series, scoring a record 974 runs, including one century, two double centuries and one triple century, a massive score of 334 at Leeds which including 309 runs in a day. Jackson died of tuberculosis at the age of 23 three years later, after playing eight Tests. The team was widely considered unstoppable, winning nine of its next ten Tests.

The 1932–33 England tour of Australia is considered one of the most infamous episodes of cricket, due to the England team's use of bodyline, where captain Douglas Jardine instructed his bowlers Bill Voce and Harold Larwood to bowl fast, short-pitched deliveries aimed at the bodies of the Australian batsmen. The tactic, although effective, was widely considered by Australian crowds as vicious and unsporting. Injuries to Bill Woodfull, who was struck over the heart, and Bert Oldfield, who received a fractured skull (although from a non-bodyline ball), exacerbated the situation, almost causing a full-scale riot from the 50 000 fans at the Adelaide Oval for the third Test.

The conflict almost escalated into a diplomatic incident between the two countries, as leading Australian political figures, including the Governor of South Australia, Alexander Hore-Ruthven, protested to their English counterparts. The series ended in a 4–1 win for England but the bodyline tactics used were banned the year after.

The Australian team put the result of this series behind them, winning their next tour of England in 1934. The team was led by Bill Woodfull on his final tour and was notably dominated by Ponsford and Bradman, who twice put on partnerships of over 380 runs, with Bradman once again scoring a triple-century at Leeds. The bowling was dominated by the spin pair of Bill O'Reilly and Clarrie Grimmett, who took 53 wickets between them, with O'Reilly twice taking seven-wicket hauls.

Sir Donald Bradman is widely considered the greatest batsman of all time. He dominated the sport from 1930 until his retirement in 1948, setting new records for the highest score in a Test innings (334 vs England at Headingley in 1930), the most runs (6996), the most centuries (29), the most double centuries and the highest Test and first-class batting averages. His record for the highest Test batting average – 99.94 – has never been beaten. It is almost 40 runs per innings above the next highest average. He would have finished with an average of over 100 runs per innings if he had not been dismissed for a duck in his last Test. He was knighted in 1949 for services to cricket. He is generally considered one of Australia's greatest sporting heroes.

Test cricket was again interrupted by war, with the last Test series in 1938 made notable by Len Hutton scoring a world record 364 for England, with Chuck Fleetwood-Smith conceding 298 runs in England's world record total of 7/903. Ross Gregory, a notable young batsman who played two Tests before the war, was killed in the war.

- Australian cricket from 1945–46 to 1960

The team continued its success after the end of the Second World War, with the first Test (also Australia's first against New Zealand) being played in the 1945–46 season against New Zealand. Australia was by far the most successful team of the 1940s, being undefeated throughout the decade, winning two Ashes series against England and its first Test series against India. The team capitalised on its ageing stars Bradman, Sid Barnes, Bill Brown and Lindsay Hassett while new talent, including Ian Johnson, Don Tallon, Arthur Morris, Neil Harvey, Bill Johnston and the fast bowling pair of Ray Lindwall and Keith Miller, who all made their debut in the latter half of the 1940s, and were to form the basis of the team for a good part of the next decade. The team that Don Bradman led to England in 1948 gained the moniker The Invincibles, after going through the tour without losing a single game.

Of 31 first-class games played during the tour, they won 23 and drew 8, including winning the five-match Test series 4–0, with one draw. The tour was particularly notable for the fourth Test of the series, in which Australia won by seven wickets chasing a target of 404, setting a new record for the highest run chase in Test cricket, with Arthur Morris and Bradman both scoring centuries, as well as for the final Test in the series, Bradman's last, where he finished with a duck in his last innings after needing only four runs to secure a career average of 100.

Australia was less successful in the 1950s, losing three consecutive Ashes series to England, including a horrendous 1956 Tour of England, where the 'spin twins' Laker and Lock destroyed Australia, taking 61 wickets between them, including Laker taking 19 wickets in the game (a first-class record) at Headingley, a game dubbed Laker's Match.

However, the team rebounded to win five consecutive series in the latter half of the 1950s, first under the leadership of Ian Johnson, then Ian Craig and Richie Benaud. The series against the West Indies in the 1960–61 season was notable for the Tied Test in the first game at the Gabba, which was the first in Test cricket. Australia ended up winning the series 2–1 after a hard-fought series that was praised for its excellent standards and sense of fair play. Stand-out players in that series as well as through the early part of the 1960s were Richie Benaud, who took a then-record number of wickets as a leg-spinner and who also captained Australia in 28 Tests, including 24 without defeat; Alan Davidson, who was a notable fast-bowler and also became the first player to take 10 wickets and make 100 runs in the same game in the first Test; Bob Simpson, who also later captained Australia for two different periods of time; Colin McDonald, the first-choice opening batsman for most of the 1950s and early '60s; Norm O'Neill, who made 181 in the Tied Test; Neil Harvey, towards the end of his long career; and Wally Grout, an excellent wicket-keeper who died at the age of 41.

- World Series Cricket and Restructuring

The Centenary Test was played in March 1977 at the MCG to celebrate 100 years since the first Test was played. Australia won the match by 45 runs, an identical result to the first Test match.

In May 1977, Kerry Packer announced he was organising a breakaway competition – World Series Cricket (WSC) – after the Australian Cricket Board (ACB) refused to accept Channel Nine's bid to gain exclusive television rights to Australia's Test matches in 1976. Packer secretly signed leading international cricketers to his competition, including 28 Australians. Almost all of the Australian Test team at the time were signed to WSC – notable exceptions including Gary Cosier, Geoff Dymock, Kim Hughes and Craig Serjeant – and the Australian selectors were forced to pick what was generally considered a third-rate team from players in the Sheffield Shield. Former player Bob Simpson, who had retired 10 years previously after a conflict with the board, was recalled at the age of 41 to captain Australia against India. Jeff Thomson was named deputy in a team that included seven debutants. Australia managed to win the series 3–2, mainly thanks to the batting of Simpson, who scored 539 runs, including two centuries; and the bowling of Wayne Clark, who took 28 wickets.

Australia lost the next series 3–1 against the West Indies, which was fielding a full strength team; and also lost the 1978–79 Ashes series 5–1, the team's worst Ashes result in Australia. Graham Yallop was named as captain for the Ashes, with Kim Hughes taking over for the 1979–80 tour of India. Rodney Hogg took 41 wickets in his debut series, an Australian record. WSC players returned to the team for the 1979–80 season after a settlement between the ACB and Kerry Packer. Greg Chappell was reinstated as captain.

The underarm bowling incident of 1981 occurred when, in an ODI against New Zealand, Greg Chappell instructed his brother Trevor to bowl an underarm delivery to New Zealand batsman Brian McKechnie, with New

Zealand needing a six to tie off the last ball. The aftermath of the incident soured political relations between Australia and New Zealand, with several leading political and cricketing figures calling it "unsportsmanlike" and "not in the spirit of cricket".

Australia continued its success up until the early 1980s, built around the Chappell brothers, Dennis Lillee, Jeff Thomson and Rod Marsh. The 1980s was a period of relative mediocrity after the turmoil caused by the Rebel Tours of South Africa and the subsequent retirement of several key players. The rebel tours were funded by the South African Cricket Board to compete against its national side, which had been banned—along with many other sports, including Olympic athletes—from competing internationally, due to the South African government's racist apartheid policies. Some of Australia's best players were poached: Graham Yallop, Carl Rackemann, Terry Alderman, Rodney Hogg, Kim Hughes, John Dyson, Greg Shipperd, Steve Rixon and Steve Smith amongst others. These players were handed three-year suspensions by the Australian Cricket Board which greatly weakened the player pool for the national sides, as most were either current representative players or on the verge of gaining honours.

- Australian cricket from 1985–86 to 2000

The so-called 'Golden Era' of Australian cricket occurred around the end of the 20th century and the beginning of the 21st century. This was a period in which Australian cricket recovered from the disruption caused by World Series Cricket to create arguably the strongest Test team in history.

Under the captaincy of Allan Border and the new fielding standards put in place by new coach Bob Simpson, the team was restructured and gradually rebuilt their cricketing stocks. Some of the rebel players returned to the national side after serving their suspensions, including Trevor Hohns, Carl Rackemann and Terry Alderman. During these lean years, it was the batsmen Border, David Boon, Dean Jones, the young Steve Waugh and the bowling feats of Alderman, Bruce Reid, Craig McDermott, Merv Hughes and to a lesser extent, Geoff Lawson who kept the Australian side afloat.

With the emergence of players such as Ian Healy, Mark Taylor, Geoff Marsh, Mark Waugh, and Greg Matthews in the late 1980s, Australia was on the way back from the doldrums. Winning the Ashes in 1989, the Australians got a roll on beating Pakistan, Sri Lanka and then followed it up with another Ashes win on home soil in 1991. The Australians went on to the West Indies and had their chances but ended up losing the series. However, they bounced back and beat the Indians in their next Test series. With the retirement of the champion but defensive, Allan Border, a new era of attacking cricket had begun under the leadership of firstly Mark Taylor and then Steve Waugh.

The 1990s and early 21st century were arguably Australia's most successful periods, unbeaten in all Ashes series played bar the famous 2005 series and achieving a hat-trick of World Cups. This success has been attributed to the restructuring of the team and system by Border, successive aggressive captains, and the effectiveness of several key players, most notably Glenn McGrath, Shane Warne, Justin Langer, Matthew Hayden, Steve Waugh, Adam Gilchrist, Michael Hussey and Ricky Ponting.

- Australian cricket from 2000–01

Following the 2006–07 Ashes series which Australia won 5 nil, Australia slipped in the rankings after the retirements of key players. In the 2013/ 14 Ashes series, Australia again defeated England 5 nil and climbed back to third in the ICC International Test rankings. In February/March 2014, Australia beat South Africa, the number 1 team in the world, 2–1 and overtook them to return to the top of the rankings. In 2015, Australia won the World Cup, losing just one game for the tournament.

As of December 2020, Australia are ranked first in the ICC Test Championship, fourth in the ICC ODI Championship and second in the ICC T20I Championship.

- 2018 Australian ball-tampering scandal

On 25 March 2018, during the third Test match against hosts South Africa; players Cameron Bancroft, Steve Smith, David Warner and the leadership group of the team were implicated in a ball tampering scandal. Smith and Bancroft admitted to conspiring to alter the condition of the ball by rubbing it with a piece of adhesive tape containing abrasive granules picked up from the ground (it was later revealed that sandpaper was used). Smith stated that the purpose was to gain an advantage by unlawfully changing the ball's surface in order to generate reverse swing.

Bancroft had been filmed tampering with the ball and after being informed he had been caught, he was seen to transfer a yellow object from a pocket to the inside front of his trousers to hide the evidence. Steve Smith and David Warner were stood down as captain and vice-captain during the third Test while head coach, Darren Lehmann was suspected to have assisted Cameron Bancroft to tamper the ball.

The ICC imposed a one-match ban and 100%-match-fee fine on Smith, while Bancroft was fined 75 per cent of his match fee and received 3 demerit points. Smith and Warner were both stripped of their captaincy roles by Cricket Australia and sent home from the tour (along with Bancroft). Tim Paine was appointed as captain for the fourth Test. Cricket Australia then suspended Smith and Warner from playing for 12 months and Bancroft for 9 months. Smith and Bancroft could not be considered for leadership roles for 12 months after the suspension, while Warner is banned from leadership of any Cricket Australia team for life.

In the aftermath of these events, Darren Lehmann announced his resignation as head coach at the end of the series with Justin Langer replacing him. On 8 May 2018, Tim Paine was also named as the ODI captain while Aaron Finch was reinstated as T20I captain hours later, although Finch replaced Paine as the ODI captain after the 5-0 ODI series whitewash in England in June 2018.

On 7 October 2018, Australia played their first Test match under new coach Justin Langer and a new leadership group, which included Tim Paine as Australia's 46th Test captain. After a 1–0 loss to Pakistan in a two match Test series against Pakistan in the UAE and a 2–1 defeat against India in a four match Test series, they found success against Sri Lanka, winning the two Test match series 2–0.

In 2019, Australia played in the Cricket World Cup, where they finished second in the group stage before being knocked out by England at Edgbaston in the semi-final. Australia went on to retain the Ashes during the 2019 Ashes series, the first time on English soil since 2001, by winning the fourth Test at Old Trafford.

In 2020–21, Australia hosted India for 3 ODIs, 3 T20Is, and 4 Tests. They won the ODI series 2–1, but lost the T20I series 2–1. Then, the two teams competed for the Border-Gavaskar Trophy which saw one of the greatest overseas Test triumphs by India in the 4th Test to win the series 2–1 with the 3rd Test being drawn.

- Team colours

For Test matches, the team wears Cricket Whites, with an optional sweater or sweater-vest with a green and gold V-neck for use in cold weather. The sponsor's (currently Alinta for home matches and Qantas for away matches) logo is displayed on the right side of the chest while the Cricket Australia emblem is displayed on the left. If the sweater is being worn the Cricket Australia emblem is displayed under the V-neck and the sponsor's logo is again displayed on the right side of the chest. The baggy green, the Australian Test cricket cap, is considered an essential part of the cricketing uniform and as a symbol of the national team, with new players being presented with one upon their selection in the team. The cap and the helmet both prominently display the Australian cricketing coat-of-arms instead of the Cricket Australia emblem. At the end of 2011, ASICS was named the manufacturer of the whites and limited over uniforms from Adidas, with the ASICS logo being displayed on the shirt and pants. Players may choose any manufacturer for their other gear (bat, pads, shoes, gloves, etc.).

In One Day International (ODI) cricket and Twenty20 International cricket, the team wears uniforms usually coloured green and gold, the national colours of Australia. There has been a variety of different styles and layouts used in both forms of the limited-overs game, with coloured clothing (sometimes known as "pyjamas") being introduced for World Series Cricket in the late 1970s. The Alinta or Qantas logo is prominently displayed on the shirts and other gears. The current home ODI kit consists of green as the primary colour and gold as the secondary colour. The away kit is the opposite of the home kit with gold as the primary colour and green as the secondary colour. The home Twenty20 kit consists of black with the natural colours of Australia, green and gold strips. However, since Australia beat New Zealand at the MCG in the 2015 Cricket World Cup wearing the gold uniform, it has also become their primary colour, with the hats used being called 'floppy gold', formerly known as 'baggy gold', a limited-overs equivalent to a baggy green. Until the early 2000s and briefly in early 2020, in ODIs, Australia wore yellow helmets, before using green helmets as in test matches.

Former suppliers were Asics (1999), ISC (2000–2001), Fila (2002–2003) and Adidas (2004–2010) among others. Before Travelex, some of the former sponsors were Coca-Cola (1993–1998), Fly Emirates (1999) and Carlton & United Breweries (2000–2001).

- match records

- Team

1. Australia is the most successful Test team in cricketing history. It has won more than 350 Test matches at a rate of almost 47%. The next best performance is by South Africa at 37%.
2. Australia have been involved in the only two Tied Tests played. The first occurred in December 1960, against the West Indies in Brisbane.The second occurred in September 1986, against India in Madras (Chennai).
3. Australia's largest victory in a Test match came on 24 February 2002. Australia defeated South Africa by an innings and 360 runs in Johannesburg.
4. Australia holds the record for the most consecutive wins with 16. This has been achieved twice; from October 1999 to February 2001 and from December 2005 to January 2008.
5. Australia shares the record for the most consecutive series victories winning 9 series from October 2005 to June 2008. This record is shared with England.
6. Australia's highest total in a Test match innings was recorded in Kingston, Jamaica against the West Indies in June 1955. Australia posted 758/8 in their first innings, with five players scoring a century.
7. Australia's lowest total in a Test match innings was recorded in Birmingham against England in May 1902. Australia were bowled all out for 36.
8. Australia are the only team to have lost a Test match after enforcing the follow-on, having been the losing side in all three such matches
9. The first Test in the 1894–95 Ashes.
10. The third Test of the 1981 Ashes.
11. The second Test in the 2000–01 Border-Gavaskar Trophy series against India.
12. Against India in March 2013, Australia became the first team in Test history to declare in their first innings and then lose by an innings.
13. In the 2013–14 Ashes series, Australia took all 100 wickets on offer in the 5–0 sweep over England.
14. Ricky Ponting and Steve Waugh have played in the most Test matches for Australia, both playing in 168 matches.

- Batting

1. Charles Bannerman faced the first ball in Test cricket, scored the first runs in Test cricket and also scored the first Test century.
2. Charles Bannerman also scored 67.34% of the Australian first innings total in match 1. This record remains to this day as the highest percentage of a completed innings total that has been scored by a single batsman.
3. Ricky Ponting has scored the most runs for Australia in Test cricket with 13,378 runs. Allan Border is second with 11,174 runs in 265 innings a record which was broken by Brian Lara during his innings of 226 against Australia while Steve Waugh has 10,927 in 260 innings. Allan Border was the first Australian batsman to pass 10,000 and the first ever batsman to pass 11,000 Test runs. Ricky Ponting was the first Australian batsman to pass 12,000 and 13,000 Test runs.
4. Matthew Hayden holds the record for the most runs in a single innings by an Australian with 380 in the first Test against Zimbabwe in Perth in October 2003.
5. Donald Bradman holds the record for the highest average by an Australian (or any other) cricketer of 99.94 runs per dismissal. Bradman played 52 Tests, scoring 29 centuries and a further 13 fifties.
6. Ricky Ponting holds the record for the most centuries by an Australian cricketer with 41. Former Australian captain Steve Waugh is in second position with 32 centuries from 260 innings.
7. Allan Border holds the record for the most fifties by an Australian cricketer with 63 in 265 innings.
8. Adam Gilchrist holds the record for the fastest century by an Australian.
9. Glenn McGrath holds the record for the most ducks by an Australian cricketer with 35 in 138 innings.

- Bowling

1. Billy Midwinter picked up the first five-wicket haul in a Test innings in match 1.
2. Fred Spofforth performed Test cricket's first hat-trick by dismissing Vernon Royle, Francis McKinnon and Tom Emmett in successive balls.
3. Fred Spofforth also took the first 10-wicket match haul in Test cricket.

4. Shane Warne holds the record for the most wickets by an Australian cricketer with 708 wickets in 145 Test matches.
5. Arthur Mailey holds the record for the best bowling figures in an innings by an Australian cricketer with 9/121 against England in February 1921.
6. Bob Massie holds the record for the best bowling figures in a match by an Australian cricketer with 16/137 against England in June 1972. That was also his first Test match for Australia.
7. J. J. Ferris holds the record for the best bowling average by an Australian bowler, taking 61 wickets at 12.70 in his career.
8. Clarrie Grimmett holds the record for the most wickets in a Test series with 44 against South Africa in 1935–36.

- Fielding and wicketkeeping

1. Ricky Ponting holds the record for the most catches in a career by an Australian fielder with 196 in 168 matches.
2. Jack Blackham performed the first stumping in Test cricket in match 1.
3. Adam Gilchrist holds the record for the most dismissals in a career by an Australian wicketkeeper with 416 in 96 matches.

- Team

1. Australia's highest total in a One-Day International innings is 434/4, scored off 50 overs against South Africa in Johannesburg on 12 March 2006. This was a world record score before the South Africans later surpassed it in the same match.
2. Australia's lowest total in a One-Day International innings is 70. This score has occurred twice; once against England in 1977 and once against New Zealand in 1986.
3. Australia's largest victory in One-Day International cricket is 275 runs. This occurred against Afghanistan at the 2015 World Cup in Australia.
4. Australia are the only team in the history of the World Cup to win 3 consecutive tournaments; 1999, 2003 and 2007.
5. Australia went undefeated at the World Cup for a record 34 consecutive matches. After being defeated by Pakistan in 1999, Australia would remain unbeaten until they were again defeated by Pakistan in 2011.
6. Australia have won the most World Cups – 5.

CHAPTER THREE

Let's Know About Cricket

- Cricket

Cricket is a bat-and-ball game played between two teams of eleven players on a field at the centre of which is a 22-yard (20-metre) pitch with a wicket at each end, each comprising two bails balanced on three stumps. The game proceeds when a player on the fielding team, called the bowler, "bowls" (propels) the ball from one end of the pitch towards the wicket at the other end. The batting side's players score runs by striking the bowled ball with a bat and running between the wickets, while the bowling side tries to prevent this by keeping the ball within the field and getting it to either wicket, and dismiss each batter (so they are "out"). Means of dismissal include being bowled, when the ball hits the stumps and dislodges the bails, and by the fielding side either catching a hit ball before it touches the ground, or hitting a wicket with the ball before a batter can cross the crease line in front of the wicket to complete a run. When ten batters have been dismissed, the innings ends and the teams swap roles. The game is adjudicated by two umpires, aided by a third umpire and match referee in international matches.

Forms of cricket range from Twenty20, with each team batting for a single innings of 20 overs and the game generally lasting three hours, to Test matches played over five days. Traditionally cricketers play in all-white kit, but in limited overs cricket they wear club or team colours. In addition to the basic kit, some players wear protective gear to prevent injury caused by the ball, which is a hard, solid spheroid made of compressed leather with a slightly raised sewn seam enclosing a cork core layered with tightly wound string.

The earliest reference to cricket is in South East England in the mid-16th century. It spread globally with the expansion of the British Empire, with the first international matches in the second half of the 19th century. The game's governing body is the International Cricket Council (ICC), which has over 100 members, twelve of which are full members who play Test matches. The game's rules, the Laws of Cricket, are maintained by Marylebone Cricket Club (MCC) in London. The sport is followed primarily in South Asia, Australasia, the United Kingdom, southern Africa and the West Indies.Women's cricket, which is organised and played separately, has also achieved international standard. The most successful side playing international cricket is Australia, which has won seven One Day International trophies, including five World Cups, more than any other country and has been the top-rated Test side more than any other country.

- History of cricket to 1725

A medieval "club ball" game involving an underhand bowl towards a batter. Ball catchers are shown positioning themselves to catch a ball. Detail from the Canticles of Holy Mary, 13th century.

Cricket is one of many games in the "club ball" sphere that basically involve hitting a ball with a hand-held implement; others include baseball (which shares many similarities with cricket, both belonging in the more specific bat-and-ball games category), golf, hockey, tennis, squash, badminton and table tennis. In cricket's case, a key difference is the existence of a solid target structure, the wicket (originally, it is thought, a "wicket gate" through which sheep were herded), that the batter must defend. The cricket historian Harry Altham identified three "groups" of "club ball" games: the "hockey group", in which the ball is driven to and fro between two targets (the goals); the "golf group", in which the ball is driven towards an undefended target (the hole); and the "cricket group", in which "the ball is aimed at a mark (the wicket) and driven away from it".

It is generally believed that cricket originated as a children's game in the south-eastern counties of England, sometime during the medieval period.Although there are claims for prior dates, the earliest definite reference to cricket being played comes from evidence given at a court case in Guildford in January 1597 (Old Style), equating to January 1598 in the modern calendar. The case concerned ownership of a certain plot of land and the court heard the testimony of a 59-year-old coroner, John Derrick, who gave witness that.

Being a scholler in the ffree schoole of Guldeford hee and diverse of his fellows did runne and play there at creckett and other plaies.

Given Derrick's age, it was about half a century earlier when he was at school and so it is certain that cricket was being played c. 1550 by boys in Surrey. The view that it was originally a children's game is reinforced by Randle Cotgrave's 1611 English-French dictionary in which he defined the noun "crosse" as "the crooked staff wherewith boys play at cricket" and the verb form "crosser" as "to play at cricket".

One possible source for the sport's name is the Old English word "cryce" (or "cricc") meaning a crutch or staff. In Samuel Johnson's Dictionary, he derived cricket from "cryce, Saxon, a stick". In Old French, the word "criquet" seems to have meant a kind of club or stick. Given the strong medieval trade connections between south-east England and the County of Flanders when the latter belonged to the Duchy of Burgundy, the name may have been derived from the Middle Dutch (in use in Flanders at the time) "krick"(-e), meaning a stick (crook). Another possible source is the Middle Dutch word "krickstoel", meaning a long low stool used for kneeling in church and which resembled the long low wicket with two stumps used in early cricket. According to Heiner Gillmeister, a European language expert of Bonn University, "cricket" derives from the Middle Dutch phrase for hockey, met de (krik ket)sen (i.e., "with the stick chase"). Gillmeister has suggested that not only the name but also the sport itself may be of Flemish origin.

- Growth of amateur and professional cricket in England

Evolution of the cricket bat. The original "hockey stick" (left) evolved into the straight bat from c. 1760 when pitched delivery bowling began.

Although the main object of the game has always been to score the most runs, the early form of cricket differed from the modern game in certain key technical aspects; the North American variant of cricket known as wicket retained many of these aspects. The ball was bowled underarm by the bowler and along the ground towards a batter armed with a bat that in shape resembled a hockey stick; the batter defended a low, two-stump wicket; and runs were called notches because the scorers recorded them by notching tally sticks.

In 1611, the year Cotgrave's dictionary was published, ecclesiastical court records at Sidlesham in Sussex state that two parishioners, Bartholomew Wyatt and Richard Latter, failed to attend church on Easter Sunday because they were playing cricket. They were fined 12d each and ordered to do penance.This is the earliest mention of adult participation in cricket and it was around the same time that the earliest known organised inter-parish or village match was played – at Chevening, Kent. In 1624, a player called Jasper Vinall died after he was accidentally struck on the head during a match between two parish teams in Sussex.

Cricket remained a low-key local pursuit for much of the 17th century. It is known, through numerous references found in the records of ecclesiastical court cases, to have been proscribed at times by the Puritans before and during the Commonwealth. The problem was nearly always the issue of Sunday play as the Puritans considered cricket to be "profane" if played on the Sabbath, especially if large crowds or gambling were involved.

According to the social historian Derek Birley, there was a "great upsurge of sport after the Restoration" in 1660. Gambling on sport became a problem significant enough for Parliament to pass the 1664 Gambling Act, limiting stakes to £100 which was, in any case, a colossal sum exceeding the annual income of 99% of the population. Along with prizefighting, horse racing and blood sports, cricket was perceived to be a gambling sport.Rich patrons made matches for high stakes, forming teams in which they engaged the first professional players.By the end of the century, cricket had developed into a major sport that was spreading throughout England and was already being taken abroad by English mariners and colonisers – the earliest reference to cricket overseas is dated 1676. A 1697 newspaper report survives of "a great cricket match" played in Sussex "for fifty guineas apiece" – this is the earliest known contest that is generally considered a First Class match.

- The patrons, and other players from the social class known as the "gentry", began to classify themselves as "amateurs" to establish a clear distinction from the professionals, who were invariably members of the working class, even to the point of having separate changing and dining facilities. The gentry, including such high-ranking nobles as the Dukes of Richmond, exerted their honour code of noblesse oblige to claim rights of leadership in any sporting contests they took part in, especially as it was necessary for them to play alongside their "social inferiors" if they were to win their bets. In time, a perception took hold that the typical amateur who played in first-class cricket, until 1962 when amateurism was abolished, was someone with a public school education who had then gone to one of Cambridge or Oxford University – society insisted that such people were "officers and gentlemen" whose destiny was to provide leadership. In a purely financial sense, the cricketing amateur would theoretically claim expenses for playing while his professional counterpart played under contract and was paid a wage or match fee; in practice, many amateurs claimed more than actual expenditure and the derisive term "shamateur" was coined to describe the practice.

- The Young Cricketer, 1768

The game underwent major development in the 18th century to become England's national sport.Its success was underwritten by the twin necessities of patronage and betting. Cricket was prominent in London as early as 1707 and, in the middle years of the century, large crowds flocked to matches on the Artillery Ground in Finsbury. The single wicket form of the sport attracted huge crowds and wagers to match, its popularity peaking in the 1748 season. Bowling underwent an evolution around 1760 when bowlers began to pitch the ball instead of rolling or skimming it towards the batter. This caused a revolution in bat design because, to deal with the bouncing ball, it was necessary to introduce the modern straight bat in place of the old "hockey stick" shape.

The Hambledon Club was founded in the 1760s and, for the next twenty years until the formation of Marylebone Cricket Club (MCC) and the opening of Lord's Old Ground in 1787, Hambledon was both the game's greatest club and its focal point. MCC quickly became the sport's premier club and the custodian of the Laws of Cricket. New Laws introduced in the latter part of the 18th century included the three stump wicket and leg before wicket (lbw).

The 19th century saw underarm bowling superseded by first roundarm and then overarm bowling. Both developments were controversial.Organisation of the game at county level led to the creation of the county clubs, starting with Sussex in 1839. In December 1889, the eight leading county clubs formed the official County Championship, which began in 1890.

The most famous player of the 19th century was W. G. Grace, who started his long and influential career in 1865. It was especially during the career of Grace that the distinction between amateurs and professionals became blurred by the existence of players like him who were nominally amateur but, in terms of their financial gain, de facto professional. Grace himself was said to have been paid more money for playing cricket than any professional.

The last two decades before the First World War have been called the "Golden Age of cricket". It is a nostalgic name prompted by the collective sense of loss resulting from the war, but the period did produce some great players and memorable matches, especially as organised competition at county and Test level developed.

- Cricket becomes an international sport

In 1844, the first-ever international match took place between the United States and Canada. In 1859, a team of English players went to North America on the first overseas tour. Meanwhile, the British Empire had been instrumental in spreading the game overseas and by the middle of the 19th century it had become well established in Australia, the Caribbean, India, Pakistan, New Zealand, North America and South Africa.

In 1862, an English team made the first tour of Australia. The first Australian team to travel overseas consisted of Aboriginal stockmen who toured England in 1868. The first One Day International match was played on 5 January 1971 between Australia and England at the Melbourne Cricket Ground.

In 1876–77, an England team took part in what was retrospectively recognised as the first-ever Test match at the Melbourne Cricket Ground against Australia. The rivalry between England and Australia gave birth to The Ashes in 1882, and this has remained Test cricket's most famous contest. Test cricket began to expand in 1888–89 when South Africa played England.

- World cricket in the 20th century

The inter-war years were dominated by Australia's Don Bradman, statistically the greatest Test batter of all time. Test cricket continued to expand during the 20th century with the addition of the West Indies (1928),

New Zealand (1930) and India (1932) before the Second World War and then Pakistan (1952), Sri Lanka (1982), Zimbabwe (1992), Bangladesh (2000), Ireland and Afghanistan (both 2018) in the post-war period. South Africa was banned from international cricket from 1970 to 1992 as part of the apartheid boycott.

- The rise of limited overs cricket

Cricket entered a new era in 1963 when English counties introduced the limited overs variant. As it was sure to produce a result, limited overs cricket was lucrative and the number of matches increased. The first Limited Overs International was played in 1971 and the governing International Cricket Council (ICC), seeing its potential, staged the first limited overs Cricket World Cup in 1975. In the 21st century, a new limited overs form, Twenty20, made an immediate impact. On 22 June 2017, Afghanistan and Ireland became the 11th and 12th ICC full members, enabling them to play Test cricket.

- A typical cricket field.

In cricket, the rules of the game are specified in a code called The Laws of Cricket (hereinafter called "the Laws") which has a global remit. There are 42 Laws (always written with a capital "L"). The earliest known version of the code was drafted in 1744 and, since 1788, it has been owned and maintained by its custodian, the Marylebone Cricket Club (MCC) in London.

- Playing area

Cricket is a bat-and-ball game played on a cricket field between two teams of eleven players each. The field is usually circular or oval in shape and the edge of the playing area is marked by a boundary, which may be a fence, part of the stands, a rope, a painted line or a combination of these; the boundary must if possible be marked along its entire length.

In the approximate centre of the field is a rectangular pitch (see image, below) on which a wooden target called a wicket is sited at each end; the wickets are placed 22 yards (20 m) apart. The pitch is a flat surface 10 feet (3.0 m) wide, with very short grass that tends to be worn away as the game progresses (cricket can also be played on artificial surfaces, notably matting). Each wicket is made of three wooden stumps topped by two bails.

• Cricket pitch and creases

As illustrated above, the pitch is marked at each end with four white painted lines: a bowling crease, a popping crease and two return creases. The three stumps are aligned centrally on the bowling crease, which is eight feet eight inches long. The popping crease is drawn four feet in front of the bowling crease and parallel to it; although it is drawn as a twelve-foot line (six feet either side of the wicket), it is, in fact, unlimited in length. The return creases are drawn at right angles to the popping crease so that they intersect the ends of the bowling crease; each return crease is drawn as an eight-foot line, so that it extends four feet behind the bowling crease, but is also, in fact, unlimited in length.

Before a match begins, the team captains (who are also players) toss a coin to decide which team will bat first and so take the first innings. Innings is the term used for each phase of play in the match.In each innings, one team bats, attempting to score runs, while the other team bowls and fields the ball, attempting to restrict the scoring and dismiss the batters. When the first innings ends, the teams change roles; there can be two to four innings depending upon the type of match. A match with four scheduled innings is played over three to five days; a match with two scheduled innings is usually completed in a single day. During an innings, all eleven members of the fielding team take the field, but usually only two members of the batting team are on the field at any given time. The exception to this is if a batter has any type of illness or injury restricting his or her ability to run, in this case the batter is allowed a runner who can run between the wickets when the batter hits a scoring run or runs,though this does not apply in international cricket. The order of batters is usually announced just before the match, but it can be varied.

The main objective of each team is to score more runs than their opponents but, in some forms of cricket, it is also necessary to dismiss all of the opposition batters in their final innings in order to win the match, which would otherwise be drawn. If the team batting last is all out having scored fewer runs than their opponents, they are said to have "lost by n runs" (where n is the difference between the aggregate number of runs scored by the teams). If the team that bats last scores enough runs to win, it is said to have "won by n wickets", where n is the number of wickets left to fall. For example, a team that passes its opponents' total having lost six wickets (i.e., six of their batters have been dismissed) have won the match "by four wickets".

In a two-innings-a-side match, one team's combined first and second innings total may be less than the other side's first innings total. The team with the greater score is then said to have "won by an innings and n runs", and does not need to bat again: n is the difference between the two teams' aggregate scores. If the team batting last is all out, and both sides have scored the same number of runs, then the match is a tie; this result is quite rare in matches of two innings a side with only 62 happening in first-class matches from the earliest known instance in 1741 until January 2017. In the traditional form of the game, if the time allotted for the match expires before either side can win, then the game is declared a draw.

If the match has only a single innings per side, then a maximum number of overs applies to each innings. Such a match is called a "limited overs" or "one-day" match, and the side scoring more runs wins regardless of the number of wickets lost, so that a draw cannot occur. In some cases, ties are broken by having each team bat for a one-over innings known as a Super Over; subsequent Super Overs may be played if the first Super Over ends in a tie. If this kind of match is temporarily interrupted by bad weather, then a complex mathematical formula, known as the Duckworth–Lewis–Stern method after its developers, is often used to recalculate a new target score. A one-day match can also be declared a "no-result" if fewer than a previously agreed number of overs have been bowled by either team, in circumstances that make normal resumption of play impossible; for example, wet weather.

In all forms of cricket, the umpires can abandon the match if bad light or rain makes it impossible to continue. There have been instances of entire matches, even Test matches scheduled to be played over five days, being lost to bad weather without a ball being bowled: for example, the third Test of the 1970/71 series in Australia.

- Innings

The innings (ending with 's' in both singular and plural form) is the term used for each phase of play during a match. Depending on the type of match being played, each team has either one or two innings. Sometimes all eleven members of the batting side take a turn to bat but, for various reasons, an innings can end before they have all done so. The innings terminates if the batting team is "all out", a term defined by the Laws: "at the fall of a wicket or the retirement of a batter, further balls remain to be bowled but no further batter is available to come in". In this situation, one of the batters has not been dismissed and is termed not out; this is because he has no partners left and there must always be two active batters while the innings is in progress.

- An innings may end early while there are still two not out batters

the batting team's captain may declare the innings closed even though some of his players have not had a turn to bat: this is a tactical decision by the captain, usually because he believes his team have scored sufficient runs and need time to dismiss the opposition in their innings

the set number of overs (i.e., in a limited overs match) have been bowled

the match has ended prematurely due to bad weather or running out of time

in the final innings of the match, the batting side has reached its target and won the game.

- Overs

The Laws state that, throughout an innings, "the ball shall be bowled from each end alternately in overs of 6 balls". The name "over" came about because the umpire calls "Over!" when six balls have been bowled. At this point, another bowler is deployed at the other end, and the fielding side changes ends while the batters do not. A bowler cannot bowl two successive overs, although a bowler can (and usually does) bowl alternate overs, from the same end, for several overs which are termed a "spell". The batters do not change ends at the end of the over, and so the one who was non-striker is now the striker and vice versa. The umpires also change positions so that the one who was at "square leg" now stands behind the wicket at the non-striker's end and vice versa.

- Clothing and equipment

English cricketer W. G. Grace "taking guard" in 1883. His pads and bat are very similar to those used today. The gloves have evolved somewhat. Many modern players use more defensive equipment than were available to Grace, most notably helmets and arm guards.

The wicket-keeper (a specialised fielder behind the batter) and the batters wear protective gear because of the hardness of the ball, which can be delivered at speeds of more than 145 kilometres per hour (90 mph) and presents a major health and safety concern. Protective clothing includes pads (designed to protect the knees and shins), batting gloves or wicket-keeper's gloves for the hands, a safety helmet for the head and a box for male players inside the trousers (to protect the crotch area). Some batters wear additional padding inside their shirts and trousers such as thigh pads, arm pads, rib protectors and shoulder pads. The only fielders allowed to wear protective gear are those in positions very close to the batter (i.e., if they are alongside or in front of him), but they cannot wear gloves or external leg guards.

Subject to certain variations, on-field clothing generally includes a collared shirt with short or long sleeves; long trousers; woolen pullover (if needed); cricket cap (for fielding) or a safety helmet; and spiked shoes or boots to increase traction. The kit is traditionally all white and this remains the case in Test and first-class cricket but, in limited overs cricket, team colours are worn instead.

- Bat and ball

Two types of cricket ball, both of the same size:

i) A used white ball. White balls are mainly used in limited overs cricket, especially in matches played at night, under floodlights (left).

ii) A used red ball. Red balls are used in Test cricket, first-class cricket and some other forms of cricket (right).

The essence of the sport is that a bowler delivers (i.e., bowls) the ball from his or her end of the pitch towards the batter who, armed with a bat, is "on strike" at the other end (see next sub-section: Basic gameplay).

The bat is made of wood, usually Salix alba (white willow), and has the shape of a blade topped by a cylindrical handle. The blade must not be more than 4.25 inches (10.8 cm) wide and the total length of the bat not more than 38 inches (97 cm). There is no standard for the weight, which is usually between 2 lb 7 oz and 3 lb (1.1 and 1.4 kg).

The ball is a hard leather-seamed spheroid, with a circumference of 9 inches (23 cm). The ball has a "seam": six rows of stitches attaching the leather shell of the ball to the string and cork interior. The seam on a new ball is prominent and helps the bowler propel it in a less predictable manner. During matches, the quality of the ball deteriorates to a point where it is no longer usable; during the course of this deterioration, its behaviour in flight will change and can influence the outcome of the match. Players will, therefore, attempt to modify the ball's behaviour by modifying its physical properties. Polishing the ball and wetting it with sweat or saliva is legal, even when the polishing is deliberately done on one side only to increase the ball's swing through the air, but the acts of rubbing other substances into the ball, scratching the surface or picking at the seam are illegal ball tampering.

- Player roles

Basic gameplay: bowler to batter

During normal play, thirteen players and two umpires are on the field. Two of the players are batters and the rest are all eleven members of the fielding team. The other nine players in the batting team are off the field in the pavilion. The image with overlay below shows what is happening when a ball is being bowled and which of the personnel are on or close to the pitch.

- Return crease

In the photo, the two batters (3 & 8; wearing yellow) have taken position at each end of the pitch (6). Three members of the fielding team (4, 10 & 11; wearing dark blue) are in shot. One of the two umpires (1; wearing white hat) is stationed behind the wicket (2) at the bowler's (4) end of the pitch. The bowler (4) is bowling the ball (5) from his end of the pitch to the batter at the other end who is called the "striker". The other batter (3) at the bowling end is called the "non-striker". The wicket-keeper (10), who is a specialist, is positioned behind the striker's wicket (9) and behind him stands one of the fielders in a position called "first slip" (11). While the bowler and the first slip are wearing conventional kit only, the two batters and the wicket-keeper are wearing protective gear including safety helmets, padded gloves and leg guards (pads).

While the umpire (1) in shot stands at the bowler's end of the pitch, his colleague stands in the outfield, usually in or near the fielding position called "square leg", so that he is in line with the popping crease (7) at the striker's end of the pitch. The bowling crease (not numbered) is the one on which the wicket is located between the return creases (12). The bowler (4) intends to hit the wicket (9) with the ball (5) or, at least, to prevent the striker (8) from scoring runs. The striker (8) intends, by using his bat, to defend his wicket and, if possible, to hit the ball away from the pitch in order to score runs.

Some players are skilled in both batting and bowling, or as either or these as well as wicket-keeping, so are termed all-rounders. Bowlers are classified according to their style, generally as fast bowlers, seam bowlers or spinners. Batters are classified according to whether they are right-handed or left-handed.

• Fielding

Of the eleven fielders, three are in shot in the image above. The other eight are elsewhere on the field, their positions determined on a tactical basis by the captain or the bowler. Fielders often change position between deliveries, again as directed by the captain or bowler.

If a fielder is injured or becomes ill during a match, a substitute is allowed to field instead of him, but the substitute cannot bowl or act as a captain, except in the case of concussion substitutes in international cricket. The substitute leaves the field when the injured player is fit to return. The Laws of Cricket were updated in 2017 to allow substitutes to act as wicket-keepers.

• Bowling and dismissal

Glenn McGrath of Australia holds the world record for most wickets in the Cricket World Cup.

Most bowlers are considered specialists in that they are selected for the team because of their skill as a bowler, although some are all-rounders and even specialist batters bowl occasionally. The specialists bowl several times during an innings but may not bowl two overs consecutively. If the captain wants a bowler to "change ends", another bowler must temporarily fill in so that the change is not immediate.

A bowler reaches his delivery stride by means of a "run-up" and an over is deemed to have begun when the bowler starts his run-up for the first delivery of that over, the ball then being "in play".

Fast bowlers, needing momentum, take a lengthy run up while bowlers with a slow delivery take no more than a couple of steps before bowling. The fastest bowlers can deliver the ball at a speed of over 145 kilometres per hour (90 mph) and they sometimes rely on sheer speed to try to defeat the batter, who is forced to react very quickly.

Other fast bowlers rely on a mixture of speed and guile by making the ball seam or swing (i.e. curve) in flight. This type of delivery can deceive a batter into miscuing his shot, for example, so that the ball just touches the edge of the bat and can then be "caught behind" by the wicket-keeper or a slip fielder. At the other end of the bowling scale is the spin bowler who bowls at a relatively slow pace and relies entirely on guile to deceive the batter. A spinner will often "buy his wicket" by "tossing one up" (in a slower, steeper parabolic path) to lure the batter into making a poor shot. The batter has to be very wary of such deliveries as they are often "flighted" or spun so that the ball will not behave quite as he expects and he could be "trapped" into getting himself out. In between the pacemen and the spinners are the medium paced seamers who rely on persistent accuracy to try to contain the rate of scoring and wear down the batter's concentration.

There are nine ways in which a batter can be dismissed: five relatively common and four extremely rare. The common forms of dismissal are bowled, caught, leg before wicket (lbw), run out and stumped. Rare methods are hit wicket,hit the ball twice, obstructing the field and timed out. The Laws state that the fielding team, usually the bowler in practice, must appeal for a dismissal before the umpire can give his decision. If the batter is out, the umpire raises a forefinger and says "Out!"; otherwise, he will shake his head and say "Not out".There is, effectively, a tenth method of dismissal, retired out, which is not an on-field dismissal as such but rather a retrospective one for which no fielder is credited.

• Batting, runs and extras

The directions in which a right-handed batter, facing down the page, intends to send the ball when playing various cricketing shots. The diagram for a left-handed batter is a mirror image of this one.

Batters take turns to bat via a batting order which is decided beforehand by the team captain and presented to the umpires, though the order remains flexible when the captain officially nominates the team. Substitute batters are generally not allowed, except in the case of concussion substitutes in international cricket.

In order to begin batting the batter first adopts a batting stance. Standardly, this involves adopting a slight crouch with the feet pointing across the front of the wicket, looking in the direction of the bowler, and holding the bat so it passes over the feet and so its tip can rest on the ground near to the toes of the back foot.

A skilled batter can use a wide array of "shots" or "strokes" in both defensive and attacking mode. The idea is to hit the ball to the best effect with the flat surface of the bat's blade. If the ball touches the side of the bat it is called an "edge". The batter does not have to play a shot and can allow the ball to go through to the wicketkeeper. Equally, he does not have to attempt a run when he hits the ball with his bat. Batters do not always seek to hit the ball as hard as possible, and a good player can score runs just by making a deft stroke with a turn of the wrists or by simply "blocking" the ball but directing it away from fielders so that he has time to take a run. A wide variety of shots are played, the batter's repertoire including strokes named according to the style of swing and the direction aimed: e.g., "cut", "drive", "hook", "pull".

The batter on strike (i.e. the "striker") must prevent the ball hitting the wicket, and try to score runs by hitting the ball with his bat so that he and his partner have time to run from one end of the pitch to the other before the fielding side can return the ball. To register a run, both runners must touch the ground behind the popping crease with either their bats or their bodies (the batters carry their bats as they run). Each completed run increments the score of both the team and the striker.

- Sachin Tendulkar is the only player to have scored one hundred international centuries

The decision to attempt a run is ideally made by the batter who has the better view of the ball's progress, and this is communicated by calling: usually "yes", "no" or "wait". More than one run can be scored from a single hit: hits worth one to three runs are common, but the size of the field is such that it is usually difficult to run four or more. To compensate for this, hits that reach the boundary of the field are automatically awarded four runs if the ball touches the ground en route to the boundary or six runs if the ball clears the boundary without touching the ground within the boundary. In these cases the batters do not need to run. Hits for five are unusual and generally rely on the help of "overthrows" by a fielder returning the ball. If an odd number of runs is scored by the striker, the two batters have changed ends, and the one who was non-striker is now the striker. Only the striker can score individual runs, but all runs are added to the team's total.

Additional runs can be gained by the batting team as extras (called "sundries" in Australia) due to errors made by the fielding side. This is achieved in four ways: no-ball, a penalty of one extra conceded by the bowler if he breaks the rules; wide, a penalty of one extra conceded by the bowler if he bowls so that the ball is out of the batter's reach bye, an extra awarded if the batter misses the ball and it goes past the wicket-keeper and gives the batters time to run in the conventional way leg bye, as for a bye except that the ball has hit the batter's body, though not his bat. If the bowler has conceded a no-ball or a wide, his team incurs an additional penalty because that ball (i.e., delivery) has to be bowled again and hence the batting side has the opportunity to score more runs from this extra ball.

- Specialist roles

Captain (cricket) and Wicket-keeper
The captain is often the most experienced player in the team, certainly the most tactically astute, and can possess any of the main skillsets as a batter, a bowler or a wicket-keeper. Within the Laws, the captain has certain responsibilities in terms of nominating his players to the umpires before the match and ensuring that his players conduct themselves "within the spirit and traditions of the game as well as within the Laws".

The wicket-keeper (sometimes called simply the "keeper") is a specialist fielder subject to various rules within the Laws about his equipment and demeanour. He is the only member of the fielding side who can effect a stumping and is the only one permitted to wear gloves and external leg guards. Depending on their primary skills, the other ten players in the team tend to be classified as specialist batters or specialist bowlers. Generally, a team will include five or six specialist batters and four or five specialist bowlers, plus the wicket-keeper.

- Umpires and scorers

Umpire (cricket), Scoring (cricket), and Cricket statistics
An umpire signals a decision to the scorers
The game on the field is regulated by the two umpires, one of whom stands behind the wicket at the bowler's end, the other in a position called "square leg" which is about 15–20 metres away from the batter on strike and in line with the popping crease on which he is taking guard. The umpires have several responsibilities including adjudication on whether a ball has been correctly bowled (i.e., not a no-ball or a wide); when a run is scored; whether a batter is out (the fielding side must first appeal to the umpire, usually with the phrase "How's that?" or "Owzat?"); when intervals start and end; and the suitability of the pitch, field and weather for playing the game. The umpires are authorised to interrupt or even abandon a match due to circumstances likely to endanger the players, such as a damp pitch or deterioration of the light.

Off the field in televised matches, there is usually a third umpire who can make decisions on certain incidents with the aid of video evidence. The third umpire is mandatory under the playing conditions for Test and Limited Overs International matches played between two ICC full member countries. These matches also have a match referee whose job is to ensure that play is within the Laws and the spirit of the game.

The match details, including runs and dismissals, are recorded by two official scorers, one representing each team. The scorers are directed by the hand signals of an umpire . For example, the umpire raises a forefinger to signal that the batter is out (has been dismissed); he raises both arms above his head if the batter has hit the ball for six runs. The scorers are required by the Laws to record all runs scored, wickets taken and overs bowled; in practice, they also note significant amounts of additional data relating to the game.

A match's statistics are summarised on a scorecard. Prior to the popularisation of scorecards, most scoring was done by men sitting on vantage points cuttings notches on tally sticks and runs were originally called notches.According to Rowland Bowen, the earliest known scorecard templates were introduced in 1776 by T. Pratt of Sevenoaks and soon came into general use.It is believed that scorecards were printed and sold at Lord's for the first time in 1846.

• thank you for buy & read this book

  have a great day of your
  from : Mr Vivek Kumar Pandey

• This All Credit Goes To My Super Hero Daddy. "Always Love You dad'.